Kubernetes Application Developer

Develop Microservices and Design a Software Solution on the Cloud

Prateek Khushalani

Apress®

Kubernetes Application Developer: Develop Microservices and Design a Software Solution on the Cloud

Prateek Khushalani
Gurgaon, Haryana, India

ISBN-13 (pbk): 978-1-4842-8031-7   ISBN-13 (electronic): 978-1-4842-8032-4
https://doi.org/10.1007/978-1-4842-8032-4

Managing Director, Apress Media LLC: Welmoed Spahr
Acquisitions Editor: Aditee Mirashi
Development Editor: Laura Berendson
Coordinating Editor: Shrikant Vishwakarma
Copyeditor: Kim Burton

Cover designed by eStudioCalamar

Cover image designed by Pexels

Distributed to the book trade worldwide by Springer Science+Business Media LLC, 1 New York Plaza, Suite 4600, New York, NY 10004. Phone 1-800-SPRINGER, fax (201) 348-4505, e-mail orders-ny@springer-sbm.com, or visit www.springeronline.com. Apress Media, LLC is a California LLC and the sole member (owner) is Springer Science + Business Media Finance Inc (SSBM Finance Inc). SSBM Finance Inc is a **Delaware** corporation.

For information on translations, please e-mail booktranslations@springernature.com; for reprint, paperback, or audio rights, please e-mail bookpermissions@springernature.com, or visit http://www.apress.com/rights-permissions.

Apress titles may be purchased in bulk for academic, corporate, or promotional use. eBook versions and licenses are also available for most titles. For more information, reference our Print and eBook Bulk Sales web page at http://www.apress.com/bulk-sales.

Any source code or other supplementary material referenced by the author in this book is available to readers on GitHub via the book's product page, located at https://link.springer.com/book/10.1007/978-1-4842-8031-7.

Printed on acid-free paper

This book is for you, Dad. As you look down from heaven, I hope you're proud of your boy.

Special thanks to my wife for constantly motivating and pushing me

A big shout to the cloud-native open source community for developing and managing such powerful and complex software solutions

Table of Contents

About the Author

 **Prateek Khushalani** is a cloud architect at Google and works as a full-stack developer in developing cloud-based accelerators. Prior to Google, he worked as a software developer at IBM and as an individual contributor to the development of SDN networking of the IBM public cloud. He has worked across industries such as software, retail, and R&D prototypes, focusing on cloud computing and machine learning. At Google, he contributes to developing tools that help accelerate a customer's migration journey to Google Cloud Platform. Prateek has strong expertise in developing and designing IaaS, PaaS, and SaaS (Software as a Service) solutions for public and private clouds. He holds a bachelor's degree from the Birla Institute of Technology, Mesra. He is an open source contributor and is an active writer on tech blogs.

About the Technical Reviewer

 **Adwait Churi** is a certified Microsoft Azure solution architect and a MuleSoft certified architect, a seasoned professional with more than 12 years of experience. His information technology career includes working in the banking, financial services, insurance, LMS (learning management system), healthcare, and hospitality industries.

Adwait is passionate about learning new technologies, including cloud, integration, microservices, ETL, and DevOps. He helps organizations with software application architecture and design, performance engineering, project management, and software development. He also provides courses on Microsoft BizTalk Server, MuleSoft, and Microsoft Azure.

Introduction

Are you a geek interested in learning how applications run on the cloud? If yes, then this book is for you. This book will enhance your knowledge about cloud computing. Even if you are a newbie just starting in the cloud domain, it does not matter. This book offers detailed information about the cloud, Kubernetes, and cloud-native technologies. It also provides best practices and techniques for developing SaaS-based solutions on the cloud.

Kubernetes Application Developer primarily targets engineers from domains ranging from developers to DevOps to SREs (Site Reliability Engineering). It addresses all the common issues that every engineer must deal with in their day-to-day job.

There are two major sections to this book:

- Educate readers on the basics of the cloud and Kubernetes

- Develop SaaS-based solutions where this new knowledge is put to the test

This book follows IaC (Infrastructure as Code), CI (Continuous Integration)/CD (Continuous Deployment), and security best practices.

CHAPTER 1

What Is Cloud Computing?

The term *cloud computing* might be trending today, but it was first seen in books around 1996. If you think this term means computers flying into clouds in the sky, you must consider what happens when it rains. Computers are certainly not waterproof and would become useless.

Let's discuss cloud computing. So, Kubernetes, a.k.a. K8s, is one of the leading software solutions which enables you to run containers in a clustered fashion. I know I have already introduced many technical words. Still, to sum up, containerization is one of the core backbones of cloud computing, and Kubernetes is the leading software solution that enables the orchestration of container-based workloads. A K8 software solution can run almost anywhere—private or public data centers or hybrid clouds.

To better understand cloud computing, let's go back to the 1960s, when computers were bulky and used only to solve business problems. At that time, engineers used to access computers on a time-sharing basis for their work. As computing evolved, so did the reach of computing power to the industries and the general public. Computers have become ubiquitous, and there is a good chance you are reading an electronic version of this book instead of a hard copy. It has blended flawlessly into everyone's lives and has become an integral part of them.

© Prateek Khushalani 2022
P. Khushalani, *Kubernetes Application Developer*,
https://doi.org/10.1007/978-1-4842-8032-4_1

Every computing device has a specific capping of resources measured in terms of CPU, RAM, HDD, network bandwidth, and more. These resources have limits, so a computing device cannot do everything. To divide this load, another device can partially take some of the work, compute it, and give the answers via the Internet, which serves as the medium to communicate. This describes one of the aspects of cloud computing. One of the prominent examples of software that uses this feature is Office 365. Much of the work is delegated to a computing device that can technically be located almost anywhere in the world (see Figure 1-1).

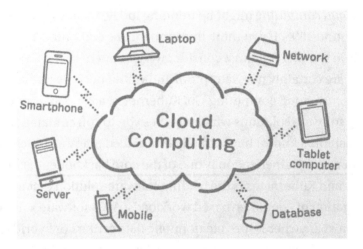

Figure 1-1. *Cloud computing overview*

Everyone is using cloud computing in one way or the other. You might be astonished to hear that you also use cloud computing every time you read an ebook. Based on the application you use, the book is cached, or part of the book is downloaded from a server (big computer) via the Internet. Thus, you are using the storage service of cloud computing, where to save the space of your computing device, only specific content is downloaded based on what you need from your library.

Computing devices such as mobiles, tablets, smartwatches, digital cars, and entry-level laptops are known as thin clients as they are portable and have limited resources. These devices need constant help from the servers running in data centers across the globe to get what you as a user demand. They constantly have some applications running which are connected to the service. Whenever these services reply with data, the device shows it as a notification.

Note   Disable your mobile data, disconnect the Wi-Fi, and then look at everything you can access on your smartphone. Is it really smart, or does it become a brick? You might not know, but even the old photos are moved to cloud storage to free up the space on your phone.

When it comes to cloud computing, there are multiple offerings. This means you can use cloud computing in different ways. However, it can be broadly categorized as follows.

- **IaaS (infrastructure as a service)** is a primary offering where the infrastructure is provided to you as a service. You can take a virtual machine or even a bare-metal server and do whatever you want to do on it. You are billed for the time you are taking the infra on rent from the cloud provider you choose. It is best suited for lift and shift, where you take the service running in your data centers and host it on the cloud.

- **PaaS (platform as a service)** offers a fully managed platform on which you can directly host your services. The tricky part is that your application needs to be made to support the platform and leverage it in the most optimum fashion. In other words, it can be an application developed and deployed on a self-managed platform to execute a time-bound task. In some PaaS-based platforms, services need to be containerized first to get them deployed. In this offering, you don't need to take care of the maintenance of the OS, patching, and other things, as you are paying for a platform and not an infrastructure.

- **SaaS (software as a service)** offers the solution on a subscription basis. The software providing the service runs on the cloud. You need to log in to it and leverage its services. The best example of this is Office 365, where all the services are running on the cloud, and you can open a browser on any thin client and create an excel or PPT. The storage interface and tools are all in the cloud. You need to create whatever you want on it from wherever you like. (You create such a solution in the final chapter of this book.)

- **iPaaS (integrated platform as a service)** is a set of automated tools that integrate software applications deployed in different environments. Large businesses that run enterprise-level systems often use iPaaS to integrate applications and data that live on-premises and public and private clouds.

- **FaaS (function as a service)** is a good solution when you don't want to care about anything but a piece of software. In this cloud offering, the developer needs to add the code in a runtime environment on a cloud. This code can then act as a function made to do a specific task triggered on any event from the client side. The cloud provider must give you all the dependencies, and you need to pay for your function.

There are more cloud offerings as well, but these are the fundamental ones, and most of the applications on the cloud today are hosted on one of these offerings. Ultimately cloud computing is a hassle-free technology. You offload your work to a set of machines not running on your premises but somewhere else to achieve a specific task. You only need to pay for the time your task was running, and once it's done, you don't need to care about anything.

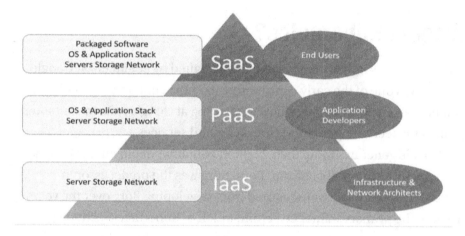

Figure 1-2. *Cloud computing offerings*

One myth to be busted in cloud computing, which is very common, is that if you lift and shift your application from your data center to a cloud, you might not see any cost benefits for scalability. This is because lift and shift is a concept where to kick off, you create precisely the same environment you have in your data center for your software solution. Then, you place the software stack as it is. This won't do any magic, but it gets your software a "Runs on the cloud" tag. The plan is to understand that it's an iterative process where you slowly and steadily convert your software solution to adapt to the cloud environment. Finally, your software reaches a maturity stage where it can leverage the full potential of its environment and be robust, scalable, cost-effective, smart, self-monitored, and intelligent.

This tells you about cloud computing, where it fits in, and what it does. Also, it tells you some of the pieces which make up cloud computing and gives an idea to the user about the various ways you can leverage the cloud. Now that you know what cloud computing is, and Kubernetes powers most of the workloads running on the cloud, let's dive directly into the main motive of this book, which is detailed knowledge about what exactly Kubernetes is and how it functions.

What Is Kubernetes?

Kubernetes was initially developed and designed by engineers at Google. Google was one of the early contributors to Linux container technology and has talked publicly about how everything at Google runs in containers. (This is the technology behind Google's cloud services.)

Google generates more than 2 billion container deployments a week, powered by its internal platform, Borg. Borg was the predecessor to Kubernetes, and the lessons learned from developing Borg over the years became the primary influence behind much of Kubernetes technology.

Kubernetes is an open source software solution that helps run containers in a cluster environment. It is a container orchestration engine responsible for managing the lifecycle of containers. Also known as K8s, it is one of the most popular and widely used software solutions to manage containers in the cloud.

Imagine that you create software that does bookkeeping. This software would have a binary/executable that you need to run/start as a process. When you start this software, it complains about some dependencies which need to be present. So, you install the prerequisites to execute the software binary.

The software gets approved and needs to be installed on hundreds of computers. So you have to do the same steps of installing the prerequisite and running the binary. Now there are the following problems.

- No easy shipment

- Packaging (how to get the dependencies)

- OS-specific changes (Debian/RPM–based/Windows)

Would it not be simpler if it could all be done via a single command? Containers do exactly this for you. As a developer, you package the software in a bundle (container image) and then run it on any machine via commands using a container runtime environment (CRE) like Docker.

So, in a nutshell, Docker is a CRE that creates containers. Kubernetes acts as an orchestrator of CRE and also creates a pool of multiple machines/nodes/servers, thus creating a cluster. You, as a developer, need to build an image of the application to create a container anywhere. No matter where the software runs, it would always have an image that you as a developer created, making the process homogeneous. The life of a developer is simplified to a great extent as the phrase, "it works on my machine," is gone, as in whatever way you are running in your local machine, it is running the same even in a production environment. So if you are developing a microservice that would run as a container, then saying such phrases won't make sense as they are all obsolete now. :)

You should now have a fair idea about how to package your application and create an image, but you might be asking how this image is retrieved in all the environments running across the globe. You're thinking in the right direction because one small piece is needed to finish the entire puzzle. That piece is known as a registry. Think of the registry as a storehouse whose responsibility is to store all the container images. You always find a registry in every cloud environment where the system pulls the container images. So there, you as a developer have a new responsibility on your shoulders: "Push the image of your application into a registry." Finally, this becomes a task for the developer as he/she needs to push the image to the registry every time a modification is done in software. Enter the CI/CD (continuous integration/continuous deployment) system to the rescue, where the task of sanity testing and pushing images to the registry is automatically done. CI/CD is covered in Chapter 3. Keep in mind that there is a process to do that, so you as a developer need to focus on one thing: writing good-quality code. :)

Figure 1-3. *Kubernetes*

To summarize, Kubernetes or K8s is responsible for managing the lifecycle of containers running on any of its nodes. It's safe to think that if your services are running as containers on a K8s cluster and configuration is done correctly, things like restart on failure, autoscaling based on rules, respawning to different nodes in case of a node failure, and other such things are automatically taken care of. There are numerous other things that K8s can do for you, and the goal of this book is to make you build smart code which can leverage all the features available and make your software fault-tolerant and future-proof.

Kubernetes Flavors

Kubernetes is an open source software solution, meaning an organization does not own it. Instead, it's a community of people working across the globe with an intent to contribute to the project. The license is Apache 2.0, which means you can freely use/modify/distribute it, and it does not have any warranty.

Suppose you install and set up Kubernetes on your machine from the GitHub repository. In that case, you are using the vanilla version of Kubernetes, which means that it's directly coming from the community, and there are no modifications. (This version is used in the book's exercises).

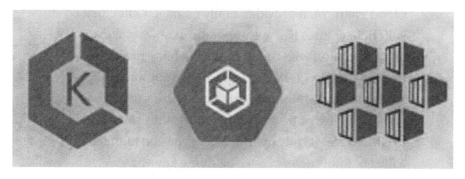

Figure 1-4. *Different flavors*

Every cloud provider has its own version of Kubernetes, and they have their own names. The following is a list of some of the popular distributions of Kubernetes.

- **Red Hat OpenShift** is one of the most popular distributions provided by Red Hat and offers a rich set of plugins for integrations with tools like Visual Studio and Eclipse. They also have their own web console and automated deployments.

- **Docker Kubernetes Service (DKS)** is one of the most popular container runtime environments. It provides its own version of Kubernetes which comes even on the Docker desktop that is very easy to install and set up. Simply install Docker for desktop, and all you need to do is toggle a button to start and play with it.

- **Rancher** is an open source container management platform built for organizations that deploy containers in production. Rancher makes it easy to run Kubernetes everywhere, meet IT requirements, and empower DevOps teams.

- **Google Kubernetes Engine (GKE)** is part of the Google Cloud Platform. It provides a fully managed K8s cluster with rich features like auto-upgrade to new versions and integration with Cloud Build–enabling practices like GitOps. Also, GKE has features like automatically scanning images stored in artifact registries to help prevent security threats. Adding the Anthos solution to GKE makes it truly hybrid, where you can manage a fleet of Kubernetes clusters running anywhere, including a public or a private cloud.

- **IBM Cloud Kubernetes Service** is part of IBM's public cloud offerings. The cluster's control plane is managed by IBM, where images are automatically scanned. IBM Watson and Blockchain services are directly accessible to containers.

- **Azure Kubernetes Service (AKS)** is Microsoft's distribution of Kubernetes hosted on the Azure cloud. It provides good integration with ADFS and Azure objects using a concept of service principles. There is also a concept of private endpoints to access different services like Cloud SQL in Azure.

- **Amazon Elastic Kubernetes Service (EKS)** provides a way to run Kubernetes on Amazon EC2 instances having ARM-based CPUs. It has its own CLI known as eksctl, which can help you set up everything hassle-free.

Whatever you choose, remember that it's all the same at the heart of everything as it's built on top of the vanilla Kubernetes cluster. The fundamentals and concepts remain the same no matter which distribution you use. It sounds like Linux, doesn't it? The distribution can be Ubuntu or Centos, but the core fundamentals are all the same.

A Bird's-eye View of the Kubernetes Architecture

Kubernetes as a software solution is complex, and Kubernetes architecture is a huge topic. However, as this book depends heavily on a K8s cluster, it is a good exercise to go through the different components inside a K8s cluster and the role of each component. Figure 1-5 illustrates the components of a Kubernetes cluster.

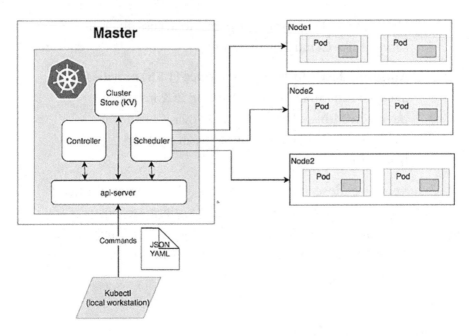

***Figure 1-5.** Kubernetes architecture*

- **Master**: The node you see on the left is the master
  node. It contains the services which make up the
  control plane of the cluster. The term control plane is
  the brain of the cluster. All the decisions ranging from
  accepting requests, validating, scheduling, and storing
  data about them are made by the components of this
  plane. Without a control plane, a cluster becomes
  headless. Let's also briefly discuss the duty of each
  component of the master node.

  - **Cluster store (KV)**: When you apply some
    configuration on a K8s cluster, it is stored here.
    etcd is an open source distributed key-store that
    K8s uses.

- **Scheduler**: When a task comes to the cluster, the scheduler decides which worker node to choose for running that task. There are a lot of algorithms relating to weighing nodes based on resources such as storage, CPU, RAM, and network, which are used to rank the nodes. The scheduler chooses the best node for the task based on the ranking value.

- **Controller**: This manages and observes if things are happening in the correct order. It is a collection of multiple processes, such as nodes, jobs, endpoints, and service account controllers. The node controller is responsible for the node's status and responds to the health of the nodes in the cluster.

- **API server**: The entry point for all the requests coming to the cluster. It's a REST-based server capable of accepting requests to the cluster.

- **NodeX**: A node is a server connected to the control plane (Master) and is used to run all the user-based workloads. **kubelet** is the service that manages the node. When a request comes to create a container, it delegates the request to the CRE, such as Docker running on the node to spawn a new container. Every node can be different in terms of hardware and even OS specifications. There can be a case when one node is running Windows OS, and another node in the same cluster is the Linux/Ubuntu type.

- **kubectl**: The command-line interface (CLI) that acts as an interface between you and the cluster. It takes the request and sends it to the API server.

Setting up a K8s Cluster

This book aims to provide hands-on experiences in Kubernetes, so you need a Kubernetes cluster to play with. There are various ways you can get a Kubernetes cluster.

- **minikube** offers one of the coolest ways to get a sandbox version of the Kubernetes cluster. Head over to `https://kubernetes.io/docs/tutorials/hello-minikube/` and hit Launch Terminal to spin up a Kubernetes cluster. The terminal pops up in the browser, and you see something similar to Figure 1-6.

Figure 1-6. *minikube*

- **kubeadm** is a CLI-based tool for setting up a cluster
  in a machine. Choose packages per your machine's
  distribution and type of operating system. The steps to

set up kubeadm are at `https://kubernetes.io/docs/`
`setup/production-environment/tools/kubeadm/`
`install-kubeadm/`.

- **Managed Kubernetes clusters**: Clouds such as GCP,
  AWS, and Azure offer managed Kubernetes solutions
  like GKE, EKS, and AKS. The cloud provider manages
  the control plane in these types of clusters.

- **Kubernetes Dashboard**: If you prefer GUI to a
  terminal, CLI might not appeal to you as an interface.
  In that case, consider a Kubernetes UI called
  Dashboard. It is not installed by default on a cluster. For
  more information on using the dashboard to control
  the cluster, head over to `https://kubernetes.io/`
  `docs/tasks/access-application-cluster/web-ui-`
  `dashboard/#deploying-the-dashboard-ui`.

Kubernetes Dashboard is shown in Figure 1-7.

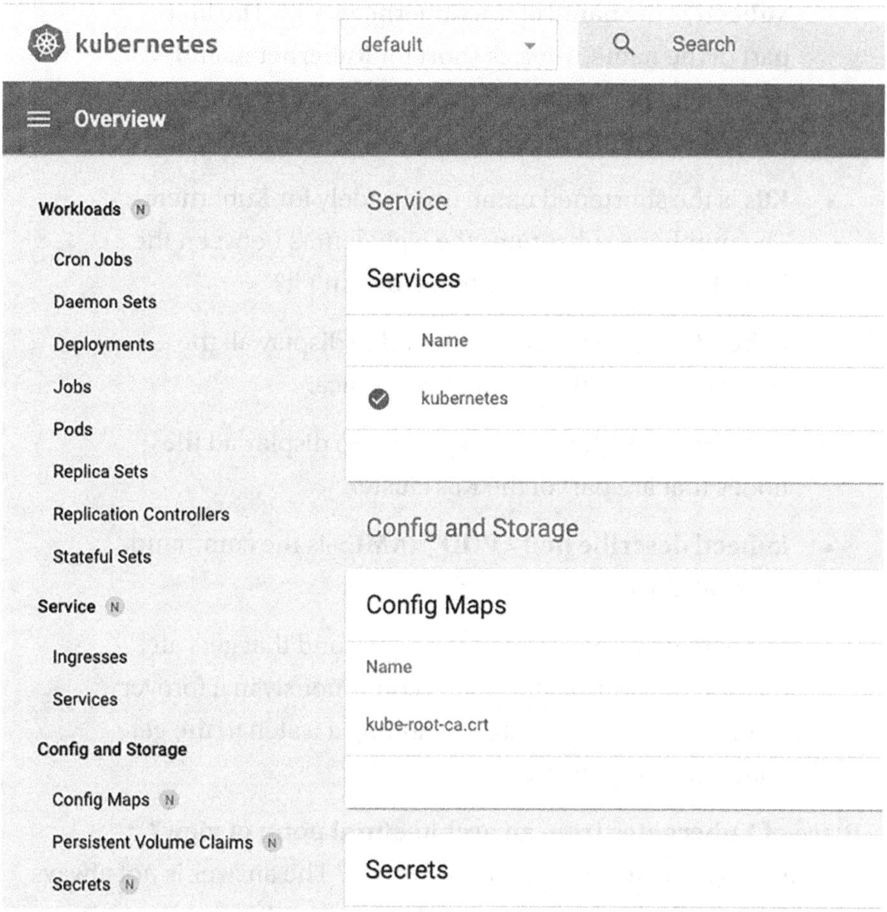

Figure 1-7. *Kubernetes Dashboard*

Common CLI Commands

Let's browse through some commonly used commands to interact with a
Kubernetes cluster. Going through the full list of commands is trivial, but
you discover new and interesting commands as you progress.

- **kubectl** is the name of the Kubernetes CLI. The first part of the name, *kube*, is short for Kubernetes, and the second part is short for *control*. This CLI lets you control your Kubernetes cluster.

- **K8s** is the shortened name used widely for Kubernetes. The number 8 substitutes the eight letters between the letter K and the letter s. Interesting, isn't it?

- **kubectl get pods** is the command to display all the pods running in the default namespace.

- **kubectl get nodes** is the command to display all the nodes that are part of the K8s cluster.

- **kubectl describe pod <POD_NAME>** is the command to get all the details of the given pod.

- **kubectl get pods —watch** is a command that gets all the pods and shows the status continuously in a forever mode until you press Ctrl+C. Adding a watch to the get commands is powerful.

Place of Kubernetes from an architectural point of view?

Where does a piece of tech fit in the puzzle? The answer is not always the same. It depends upon how you use Kubernetes. Some companies might be running K8s on bare metal, taking care of workloads running on physical machines, while some e-commerce companies might be running their Front-end tech stack on a K8s cluster powered by a bunch of virtual machines.

The possibilities are endless as Kubernetes is a container orchestration engine. The architect designing a software solution is the decision-maker and needs to decide how to use it based on the use case and suitability.

Some of the areas where containers might not be of good use are when the process needs to interact with the kernel or manage the operating system itself. The following are some cases that might help you understand the process better.

Case 1

You have to develop software that manages how many interfaces are on your host system and disable the ones getting a lot of traffic. In such a case running this service as a container might not be a good choice.

Case 2

A company wants to shift its software solutions to the cloud as soon as possible. Moving their software stack to the cloud might be trivial because it would take a lot of time that the company does not have. So, in this case, to kick off things, everything is deployed by the company on the IaaS cloud offering first. After that, they can re-architect the software solution to break everything into microservice architecture, finally making them land a K8s engine.

Case 3

You developed an online inventory management software that has only two services, performs flawlessly, and meets your organization's expectations. It is overkill to create an entire K8s cluster of three or more nodes to host this software. In addition, the CAPEX (capital expenditure) and OPEX (operating expenditure) that your organization would incur in procuring and maintaining a K8s cluster are much higher, making the software design inefficient.

The basic thumb rule that needs to be followed is that whatever can be containerized is considered the best. If it's not possible, you must stick to system processes. It's not always possible to apply the same rule in every situation as every situation is technically different. Hence, the decision to use K8s depends on the feasibility, outcome, and benefits you get.

Summary

You have learned the history of cloud computing, how it originated, and the typical offerings or models of cloud. Since this book is about developing and deploying applications on Kubernetes, it focuses more on the container solutions offered in cloud computing. Even if you are new to the concepts of Kubernetes and containers, it's perfectly okay. Ultimately, it's all related to computing, networking, monitoring, and managing systems.

Please make sure you have a running Kubernetes cluster after completing this chapter because the rest of the chapters are dependent on it. This book aims to make you aware of how things work and help you practice it yourself. By the end of this book, you should be confident in containerizing and running services on K8s on any cloud provider solution. Let's summarize the key things you learned in this chapter.

- What cloud computing is

- How cloud computing works

- What cloud computing offers

- What Kubernetes is

- How to set up Kubernetes

- Where Kubernetes fits in

CHAPTER 2

Creating Applications on Kubernetes

In the last chapter, you learned about Kubernetes, its architecture, and how and when you can use it. You also set up your own Kubernetes cluster, which will be used throughout the book. If you haven't created a cluster, I strongly recommend heading back to the previous chapter and trying to create one.

You have set up the cluster and installed a command-line interface (CLI) known as kubectl that enables you to interact with the cluster and see how it is running. With all the steps performed until now, you can only run bare minimum services that make up a cluster. It's now time to deploy some applications on the cluster, and what is better than a simple HTTP server hosting a web page? To do this, I have chosen an Apache-based HTTP server.

Note If you already have a K8s cluster hosted on a cloud, it also works because, at the heart of everything, it's the same.

© Prateek Khushalani 2022
P. Khushalani, *Kubernetes Application Developer*,
https://doi.org/10.1007/978-1-4842-8032-4_2

Let's now move to the cool and interesting part of this book: start running things on Kubernetes and play with it. You slowly start by creating small independent applications, then link them together, and finally reach a stage where every application is a small microservice running to achieve a specific task.

Create an Apache HTTP Server

An Apache HTTP server is an open source server based on HTTP protocol. It's a very simple yet powerful application that can serve as an engine on which your website runs. Figure 2-1 illustrates a basic view of an HTTP server.

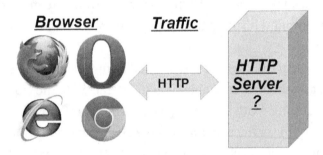

Figure 2-1. *HTTP server overview*

Before starting, let's follow the process you learned concerning containers and running them on K8s. It can be summarized as follows.

- A **container image** runs the container (what it is and how to get it).

- **CRE** is the acronym for *container runtime environment*; it is the container driver.

- **COE** is the acronym for *container orchestration engine*: it manages thousands of containers.

The Apache HTTP server is open source and not owned by any organization; hence it is freely available and can be downloaded from Docker Hub (https://hub.docker.com), a public registry provided by the Docker organization from where you can get all the popular images. However, an organization generally refrains from pulling images from Docker Hub as they have their own private registries. Private registries act as the storehouse of the images which contain the applications developed by engineering teams of an organization.

Please note that you cannot trust the images downloaded from Docker Hub, as anyone can create an account and publish their own images. To know which image is being downloaded, always remember to look at the following commands.

- **docker pull funfact** is the command that pulls the image from the Docker Hub. It finds an image with the name **funfact.** The image is official as it does not have any username before it. Therefore, you can trust this image completely.

- **docker pull Mario/funfact** is the command that pulls the image from the Docker Hub, and it finds an image with the name **Mario/funfact**. The image is *not* official as it is created by a Mario user account and should only be downloaded when you trust the user.

- **docker pull myplace.registry.com/funfact** is the command that pulls the image from a third-party registry **myplace.registry.com.** The image should be downloaded only when you are aware of this registry. Most private registries are locked, and only authorized users can download/upload images to them.

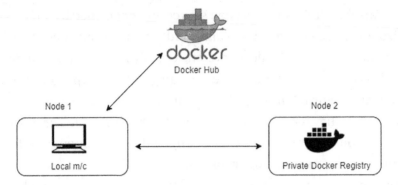

Figure 2-2. *Docker images*

This book mostly sticks to the official public images and uses Docker Hub as the storehouse for images. HTTP server's official image name is HTTPD, so the command to pull the docker image is ***docker pull httpd:2.4.46***. One thing to note here are tags, which are nothing but versions of the images. As you have given 2.4.46 after the colon, the version of this image is 2.4.46. This corresponds to the version of the server inside it.

You should be getting an output similar to this. If you get something like *manifest not found,* then it means that the image is no longer there, and you can try with some other version. Even if you don't give any version and run ***docker pull httpd***, it works, as it fetches the image from a default tag called ***latest.*** The output is similar to Figure 2-3.

```
I          @cloudshell:~$ docker pull httpd:2.4.46
2.4.46: Pulling from library/httpd
69692152171a: Pull complete
7284b4e0cc7b: Pull complete
3678b2d55ccd: Pull complete
ab492cf0b2a4: Pull complete
991f7f97a9d8: Pull complete
Digest: sha256:e4c2b93c04762468a6cce6d507d94def02ef4dc285278d0d926e09827f4857db
Status: Downloaded newer image for httpd:2.4.46
docker.io/library/httpd:2.4.46
```

Figure 2-3. *Docker pull*

You have the image for the software you need to run on your system. The code is now on your machine, waiting to be executed.

Note   What if, while pulling the image, your system crashes or the Internet goes away? The command would fail, but if you run it again once the connectivity is up, would it pull the entire image again? The answer to this is that an image comprises multiple layers, and each layer is a separate image having its own digest and sha256 signature. Only the remaining layers/images are downloaded when the command is executed again. This is one of the most powerful features of Docker.

Remember that K8s is a manager, and Docker is one of CRE's K8s supports. The steps you are doing here help you understand what K8s does, but they are not required in an actual environment. With this in mind, let's look at what happens if you start the container manually via Docker. To start the container, run ***docker run -it --rm httpd:2.4.46*** as shown in Figure 2-4.

```
cloudshell:~$ docker run -it --rm httpd:2.4.46
AH00558: httpd: Could not reliably determine the server's fully qualified domain name, using 172.18.0.2. Set the 'Server
Name' directive globally to suppress this message
AH00558: httpd: Could not reliably determine the server's fully qualified domain name, using 172.18.0.2. Set the 'Server
Name' directive globally to suppress this message
[Tue Jan 25 14:34:31.017686 2022] [mpm_event:notice] [pid 1:tid 139851983692928] AH00489: Apache/2.4.46 (Unix) configure
d -- resuming normal operations
[Tue Jan 25 14:34:31.017909 2022] [core:notice] [pid 1:tid 139851983692928] AH00094: Command line: 'httpd -D FOREGROUND'
```

Figure 2-4. *Docker run*

If you see something similar to what's shown in Figure 2-3, then congratulations, you have just successfully started the first container of this book. Though it's not doing much, that's okay. Running the command might have also taken control of your terminal. To get the control back, press Ctrl+C and it gracefully exits and comes out. The **-it** parameters mean that the containers' standard input is your keyboard. On the other hand, **-rm** means to remove the container once it is dead (garbage cleaning).

Since you don't need the image anymore, remove it via the ***docker rmi*** command, as shown in Figure 2-5.

```
:loudshell:~$ docker rmi   httpd:2.4.46
Untagged: httpd:2.4.46
Untagged: httpd@sha256:e4c2b93c04762468a6cce6d507d94def02ef
Deleted: sha256:f3cffeea581b3306a13d80b25a437f73f767b8f27af
Deleted: sha256:887d0217b7251e4d5ad46486c19c5e2c82ae8aa6d53
Deleted: sha256:e04f6a8ae4f2939d3b73fd06085169c625486a81d38
Deleted: sha256:85643304b5484a30ffe669196e71d6b763661800e12
Deleted: sha256:7524155083fa19d15b8902105916a8da484d1ff5d36
Deleted: sha256:02c055ef67f5904019f43a41ea5f099996d8e763374
```

Figure 2-5. *Docker rmi*

The following summarizes the steps.

1. Identify the name of the image to be pulled for HTTPD.

2. Pull the image from the Docker Hub.

3. Create a container for the image.

4. Terminate the container.

5. Remove the image since it's no longer required.

Wow, that's a lot of work that you did here. Pat yourself on the back. :) Now let the champ K8s enter the market, do everything for you in a single command, and steal the thunder. The command to create an HTTPD container/Pod on Kubernetes is ***kubectl run my apache --image=httpd:2.4.46***.

Once you run this command, you should get something like **Pod myapache created**. Before moving further, let's know what a Pod is and how it is different from a container. A Pod is nothing but a collection of like-minded containers. A process running inside a container might need some assistance, sometimes throughout its lifetime or when it is coming up. Also, there can be a situation where multiple processes need to be right next to each other and communicate as if they are on the same host. You can bundle multiple services into a Pod where each service runs in its own container to provide such features. Each service running inside a different container can communicate via localhost. Isn't that great?

Now let's move to the part where you check the status of the Pod. To get the status, run the **kubectl get pods myapache** command. You should get an output similar to Figure 2-6.

Note If you are new to Kubernetes, I recommend going through the cheat sheet that documents all the commonly used commands in K8s. You can find it at `https://kubernetes.io/docs/reference/kubectl/cheatsheet/`.

```
  .            _ecloudshell:~ (argon-system-337506)$ kubectl get pods myapache
NAME           READY    STATUS      RESTARTS     AGE
myapache       1/1      Running     0            2m45s    ▬
```

Figure 2-6. Get Pod status

The output of this command tells you a brief status of the Pod. Most of the output is self-explanatory. The RESTARTS column gives you the count of how many restarts of the Pod have happened until now. The AGE column tells how much time it has been since the inception of the Pod. Let's move to a more elaborative part and see more Pod details via the **kubectl describe pod myapache** command. You should see output similar to Figure 2-7 (only the last part).

```
Normal    Pulling      5m21s              kubelet      Pulling image "httpd:2.4.46"
Normal    Pulled       5m12s              kubelet      Successfully pulled image "h
ttpd:2.4.46" in 8.210282004s
Normal    Created      5m11s              kubelet      Created container myapache
Normal    Started      5m11s              kubelet      Started container myapache
```

Figure 2-7. Describe Pod

The other parts of the output are covered later in the book but for now, let's focus on the last part, which gives you the events of the Pod. To summarize the events, K8s did the things you manually performed in the earlier section: select a node on which the Pod runs, pull the image from the Docker Hub, and start the container.

Now let's access the service and check if it's working. Let's use the port-forward technique to access the Pod. Please note that this way of accessing a service running inside a Pod is only for development purposes and should not be used for production purposes. K8s forwards all the traffic coming from localhost (your machine) to the container using the port-forward technique. Try running the ***kubectl port-forward myapache 8080:80*** command, which forwards all the traffic from your machine at port 8080 to the container's port 80. Head to your browser and try accessing the server. You should see an output similar to Figure 2-8.

Figure 2-8. *Apache server*

If you see something similar to Figure 2-7, congratulations, you have successfully accessed the server. Head back to the terminal and press **Ctrl+C** to gracefully exit the port-forward utility of kubectl. Finally, use ***kubectl delete pod myapache*** to delete the Pod you created for this exercise.

Create a Java Tomcat WAR-based Server

You are now aware of how Kubernetes creates a Pod and the tasks necessary to create a Pod. The tasks that K8s does to make a Pod reach a running state are crucial to understanding because they help debug scenarios when a Pod might crash and is unable to start. As you progress towards creating other services, you can skip the steps you did manually via Docker commands because they were only for learning; they are not required.

Tomcat is another popular server for Java-based applications. It runs a Java virtual machine (JVM) and provides the rendering of Java-based web applications. Its image is available in the Docker Hub, like HTTPD. This exercise uses a *tomcat:10-jdk15* image. Let's deploy a Tomcat server on the K8s cluster via the *kubectl run mycat --image=tomcat:10-jdk15* command. Once the command is executed, K8s creates a Pod with the image specified in the command.

Based on Internet speed, the Pod might take some time to come to a running state because the image pull takes time. If you use *kubectl get pods mycat* you might see the *ContainerCreating* status, which means the container has not started yet.

If you are curious to know what K8s is doing, try running the **kubectl get events** command. As this is a command of global scope, you get a lot of information but for now, stick to the information you see at the bottom of the output. You should be seeing something similar to Figure 2-9.

```
35s          Normal    TaintManagerEviction    pod/mycat    Cancelling deletion of Pod default/mycat
34s          Normal    Pulling                 pod/mycat    Pulling image "tomcat:10-jdk15"
14s          Normal    Pulled                  pod/mycat    Successfully pulled image "tomcat:10-jdk15" in 20.418815143s
11s          Normal    Created                 pod/mycat    Created container mycat
11s          Normal    Started                 pod/mycat    Started container mycat
```

Figure 2-9. *Kubernetes events*

So now, with this output, it is pretty much clear what K8s is currently doing and exactly how much time every step has taken. Now let's make the exercise a little bit interesting. In the last exercise, you ran an HTTPD server, but you didn't host anything on it, so for Tomcat, let's add a WAR (web application archive) containing a sample web application. You can get the sample WAR file at `https://tomcat.apache.org/tomcat-7.0-doc/appdev/sample/sample.war`.

You can download the WAR file and place it somewhere on your local machine. Keep a note of the location where the WAR is present on your machine. Before proceeding, let's discuss a couple of things.

1.   The image to run the Pod is a vanilla image of the Tomcat server and does not contain the sample WAR application.

2.   You want the WAR sample application to be present inside the container for this use case. How do you do this?

One way of solving this is to create another image with Tomcat and the sample application's WAR file. But what if there is a need to change the WAR file, or there is another application (WAR file) you want to host on Tomcat? What do you do then? Create another image with that WAR file. Certainly, this approach is not scalable.

To solve this problem, you can leverage the concept of volumes in Kubernetes. Using volumes, you can mount the files you want on the Pod. This approach decouples the container image from specific application files as the image is a standard Tomcat server and the application files become part of the container via volume mounts.

Let's create a volume in K8s, which is then linked with the Pod. First, you must create a PersistentVolume in K8s. You can do this by having a YAML file similar to the following.

```
apiVersion: v1
kind: PersistentVolume
metadata:
  name: local-vol
  labels:
        type: local
spec:
  storageClassName: manual
  capacity:
        storage: 10Gi
  accessModes:
        - ReadWriteOnce
  hostPath:
        path: "<YOUR_SYSTEM_PATH_TO_MOUNT>"
```

Here you are creating a PersistentVolume (PV) that has **hostPath.**
Please note that in testing and development cases, having hostPath is
allowed, but it is not suited for production environments. As you progress,
I will explain the PV sources as well. In the **path** key, the value should be
the path of your system which you want to mount. Now run the **kubectl
create -f PV.yaml** command, where PV.yaml is the name of the YAML
file. As the PV is created, let's create a PersistentVolumeClaim (PVC) that
claims the PV you just created.

Here is a sample PVC YAML.

```
apiVersion: v1
kind: PersistentVolumeClaim
metadata:
  name: local-pv-claim
spec:
  storageClassName: manual
  accessModes:
```

```
    - ReadWriteOnce
resources:
    requests:
        storage: 3Gi
```

If you notice carefully, you find no modification required in the PVC. You can simply copy it and create it. It is the responsibility of K8s to find a PV that satisfies the requirements of this PVC. This is done by matching the storageclassName field. You can create this PVC via the **kubectl create -f PVC.yaml** command, where PVC.yaml is the name of the file having the same contents. Let's check the status of the newly created PV and PVC.

- **kubectl get PV local-vol**: In this snippet, notice the STATUS column with a Bound value, which means that some PVC claims the PV. Figure 2-10 illustrates this.

NAME	CAPACITY	ACCESS MODES	RECLAIM POLICY	STATUS	CLAIM	STORAGECLASS	REASON	AGE
local-vol	10Gi	RWO	Retain	Bound	default/local-pv-claim	manual		16m

Figure 2-10. *Persistent volume*

- **kubectl get PVC local-PV-claim**: In this snippet, notice the VOLUME column that has a local-vol value, which indicates that K8s was able to create a linking between PV and PVC via the STORAGECLASS field. Figure 2-11 illustrates this.

NAME	STATUS	VOLUME	CAPACITY	ACCESS MODES	STORAGECLASS	AGE
local-pv-claim	Bound	local-vol	10Gi	RWO	manual	7m15s

Figure 2-11. *Persistent volume claims*

You are done setting up a volume for the K8s cluster, which points to the hostPath of your local system. Let's try mounting it to the Tomcat Pod you created earlier; but you must first learn another concept. To use YAML files to create a Pod, like you created PV and PVC via YAML files instead of commands. Though using commands sounds good, consider a case when you have an application that needs to be installed on hundreds of K8s clusters. In this case, each application running on every cluster has different values and environment variables. So, you create different sets of commands for every environment, which becomes a scalability issue.

To overcome this problem, you can create a set of YAML files and a script that leverages the power of sed and awk commands. This combination can alter the values as per the environment in the YAML files. So again, your deployment system becomes scalable. :) One approach to developing such a templating system is by yourself, and the other is by using another powerful tool called Helm.

Helm is an open source tool that stores the application YAML as charts, and the values to these charts are provided during the deployment of the application. Helm repo contains numerous charts, and every chart represents an application that can deploy it on a Kubernetes cluster. Helm comes with its own CLI and is very similar to kubectl in terms of usage.

The Kubernetes ecosystem accepts the deployment of objects such as Pod via YAML-based files. These YAML files are declarative where the deployment entity, which can be a CI (continuous integration) system or an engineer, provides which application is to be deployed along with the other necessary parameters supporting the deployment.

YAML can be templated and made scalable where the values provided to the variables can be decoupled and injected via string manipulating tools such as sed or awk. You are free to maintain YAML files for your custom application or create Helm charts for them and use the Helm framework for templating.

Note   A sample Tomcat Pod was created at the beginning of the chapter. Before creating the Pod via the YAML, please delete the existing Pod via the **kubectl delete pod mycat** command.

With this learning of how YAMLs are used in the K8s ecosystem, let's create a YAML for the Tomcat Pod with PVC mounts.

```yaml
apiVersion: v1
kind: Pod
metadata:
  name: mycat
spec:
  volumes:
        - name: war-files
        persistentVolumeClaim:
        claimName: local-pv-claim
  containers:
        - name: mycat
        image: tomcat:10-jdk15
        ports:
        - containerPort: 8080
        name: "tomcat-server"
        volumeMounts:
        - mountPath: "/usr/local/tomcat/webapps"
        name: war-files
```

The following describes each field.

- **apiVersion** is the version of the Kubernetes API under which this object (Pod) is found

- **kind** is the object type for which details are provided. In this case, it is Pod.

- **metadata** contains the details like the name of the Pod. It can also contain the namespace under which the Pod should lie (Thinking about what namespaces are). It comes later in the book, so don't worry about that part. :)

- **spec** is the "meaty" part that tells about the Pod specifications. The containers section is a must, and as you want to mount the volume, you have that section as well.

  - **volumes** has the details on the PVC that needs to be used as a volume.

  - **containers** has details such as the name of the image that needs to be used for creating a container. The port section tells which container port needs to be exposed (Tomcat runs on 8080). The **volumeMounts** section takes the name of the volume that you defined in the volumes section (4.a), and mountPath tells where to mount the volume inside the container. As Tomcat reads WAR files from */usr/local/tomcat/webapps*, you have mounted the volume to that directory.

Now that you know about the Tomcat Pod YAML, and since PV and PVC were already created on the cluster, let's run the ***kubectl create -f pod.yaml*** command, where pod.yaml contains the Pod specifications.

Copy the WAR sample application you downloaded earlier to the local system directory. Remember this directory is mounted as a volume on the container. Once the Pod status shows that it is running, you are set to see everything in action. Let's use port-forward to access the Tomcat server via localhost ***kubectl port-forward mycat 8080:8080***. Head to your browser and type **http://127.0.0.1:8080/sample/**. You should see something similar to Figure 2-12.

Figure 2-12. *Sample application on Tomcat*

Congratulations! You have successfully hosted a sample application on the Tomcat server running on K8s.

It is safe to say that you know how to deploy an application on a Kubernetes cluster and mount volumes to an application using the concept of persistent volumes. But when workloads run as containers, different workloads often want to send and receive information between them. In a native programming language, this is called interprocess communication (IPC), in which one process gets the information from another process. Similar to that in the container world, when every container represents a microservice, they might want to talk to each other to share information. For such cases, you have RPC (Remote Procedure Call), where callers make a request and get a response back with some data from the receiver. gRPC is an RPC system that is very powerful, effective, language-independent, and fast.

Create a gRPC Server

Before creating a gRPC server, let's discuss gRPC and how it is different from a REST-based server. gRPC works on the concept of proto, where a user must create a file that describes the RPC and the input and output message that the RPC needs.

Consider it as a blueprint where the developer of the RPC is describing the name and attributes of the RPC. Once the developer creates a proto file, the protoc compiler can create a client and server in any required language. The following can be said about RPC.

- It is programming-language agnostic.

- It abstracts code generation because the client/server is automatically generated.

- The proto file is human readable, and comments can make it more user-friendly.

The client can be in a Python library, and the server can be in Golang. gRPC runs on HTTP2, supports TLS for security, and is eight times faster than REST. The data is not in JSON but a protocol buffer that gets converted into a message defined by the developer in the proto. Whatever message the developer creates for the RPC, the protocol buffers are serialized/deserialized accordingly. One of the downsides of this system is that the server cannot be poked via tools like CURL, which can be done in a REST server. You always need a client library for the gRPC server to communicate with it. Figure 2-13 overviews gRPC.

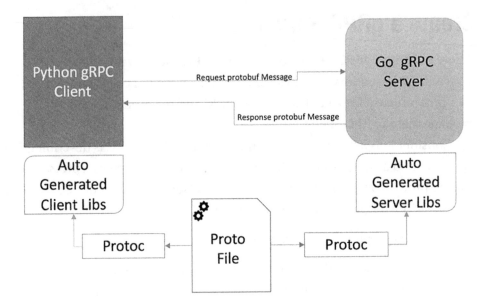

Figure 2-13. *gRPC Overview*

With these concepts in mind, let's try creating a basic gRPC server with an RPC returning a "Hello world" message when a client invokes it. This entire example can be cloned from the GitHub repository at `https://github.com/prateek2408/BookExamples/tree/main/gRPC`.

As proto is the basis on which everything works, let's try creating a proto having the following contents.

```
syntax = "proto3";
package myfirstrpc;

//A sample service which contains all our rpc.
Service MyService{
 //The definition of rpc.
 rpc MyFunc() returns (StringMessage) {}

#The message to Return when rpc is invoked.
message StringMessage {
```

```
    string  reply = 1;
}
```

This proto is simple: create a service. Inside that service, create an RPC named MyFunc, which is not taking any input. When called, it returns a StringMessage.

As the proto part is complete, let's create a server for it. For the Server, let's use Golang. Remember to convert this proto into Golang code using a *protoc compiler*. Since this book focuses on cloud practices, let's not waste time installing protoc and its dependencies. Rather let's use a docker image that has everything installed for you. Consider having a proto file named ***hello-world.proto*** in your PWD (present working directory). PWD is a special environment variable in the terminal. It contains the absolute path of the directory to which the user is currently pointing. Run the following command.

```
docker run -it --rm -v $PWD:/opt/helloworld -w /opt/helloworld
prateek2408/protoc-go
```

The image is coming from a Docker Hub and is under my username. If you are curious to know what this image contains, head over to https://github.com/prateek2408/DockerImages/blob/main/protoc-go/Dockerfile for details about it. After running this command, you land into the container, and your proto is mounted in the */opt/* directory. Run the command to generate the Go libraries for ***hello-world.proto***.

```
protoc --go_out=. --go_opt=paths=source_relative --go-
grpc_out=.  hello-world.proto
```

This command should take only a few seconds; once completed, you see a bunch of files created in the directory. The protoc part is done, and you can safely turn off your container and come up by typing **exit**.

```
total 16K
-rw-r--r-- 1 root root  353 Mar  7 13:05 hello-world.proto
-rw-r--r-- 1 root root 6.3K Mar  7 13:08 hello-world.pb.go
-rw-r--r-- 1 root root 3.4K Mar  7 13:08 hello-world_grpc.pb.go
```

Figure 2-14. *Protocol buffer output*

Figure 2-14 shows that the files created have a similar string, pb, which stands for *protocol buffer.*

Before proceeding, there is one thing to note about proto it is not glued with gRPC. Protocol buffers can be used in all the applications that support it, and gRPC is one of them. This is why you gave the flags, which included gRPC to tell protoc to generate specific gRPC libraries.

Now you are done with the automated code generation part. Let's write a ***main.go*** to call the gRPC server and start it. You can take the **main. go** file from the GitHub repository at https://github.com/prateek2408/ BookExamples/blob/main/gRPC/server/main.go.

This is a basic example where you are trying to call the gRPC server via the files created by protoc and start it insecurely at port 2408. If you have SSL certificates, you can create an SSL-enabled gRPC server. Now let's see if you can run the server you created. A Docker image builds the Go code. Let's run it.

```
docker run -it --rm -v $PWD:/opt/myrpc -w /opt/myrpc
golang bash
```

Since you are again in the Docker container shell, let's build the application via the **go build -o myserver server/main.go** command. Once the command completes, you get a binary in the directory known as **myserver**. Try executing it via **./myserver** and see if it works. If everything is successful, you see something similar to Figure 2-15.

```
[root@17cf41d6c22d:/opt/myrpc# go build -o myserver server/main.go
go: downloading google.golang.org/grpc v1.36.0
go: downloading github.com/golang/protobuf v1.4.3
go: downloading google.golang.org/protobuf v1.25.0
go: downloading google.golang.org/genproto v0.0.0-20200526211855-cb27e3aa2013
go: downloading golang.org/x/net v0.0.0-20190311183353-d8887717615a
go: downloading golang.org/x/sys v0.0.0-20190215142949-d0b11bdaac8a
go: downloading golang.org/x/text v0.3.0
[root@17cf41d6c22d:/opt/myrpc# ./myserver
[gRPC server starting at port 2408
```

Figure 2-15. *Golang server*

Congratulations, your server is up and running. Terminate it by
pressing Ctrl+C, then exit the container shell and return to your system's
environment. You have a gRPC server created by the proto. The left part
shows how to package it and run it as a container in K8s. It's time to build
an image, and for that, you need to create a Dockerfile that the Docker
utility understands.

Here are the contents of the Dockerfile.

```
FROM golang
ADD . /opt/myrpc
WORKDIR /opt/myrpc
RUN  go build -o myserver server/main.go

FROM ubuntu
WORKDIR /myrpc/
COPY  --from=0 /opt/myrpc/myserver .
EXPOSE 2408
CMD ["./myserver"]
```

Notice what was done here. It used multi-builds in Dockerfile. A multi-
build is a process in which you create an interim container for building
your project. In this case, binary is the final artifact generated. Golang is
a low-level programming language, and you need only the binary to run
an application and not the source code. The interim Docker container is
doing what you did manually to build the binary earlier.

Once the binary is built, use a Ubuntu image, which is very tiny and does not contain anything to host the binary. Build this image via the docker build -t myrpc -f Dockerfile command.

By default, docker build searches for a file named Dockerfile in your directory. If your file name is different, you can specify it by the **-f** command-line argument. It's a good practice to specify the filename to determine which file is being used for building the image.

It may take some time to build an image. Once it's completed, run the **docker images** command, and you should be able to see the image as shown in Figure 2-16.

```
myrpc latest 2d8444f980e8 5
```

Figure 2-16. *Docker image*

You have finally done it if you can see the image illustrated in Figure 2-16. You have created the first application of this book with your own hands from scratch and packaged it as a Docker container. It's never bad to verify your image, so let's run the image via the **docker run -d --name mycon myrpc** command. This creates a container in the detached mode, so your console is given back to you. Let's view the container's logs by running the ***docker logs mycon*** command. You should see logs similar to what's shown in Figure 2-17.

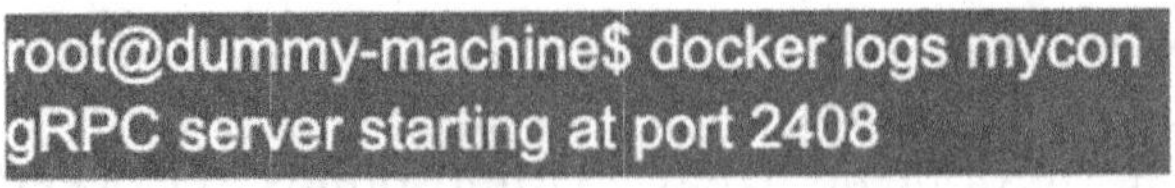

```
root@dummy-machine$ docker logs mycon
gRPC server starting at port 2408
```

Figure 2-17. *Docker container*

This shows that the gRPC server is up and running in the container. Since the verification is complete, let's delete the container via the **docker rm -f mycon** command. All verification is done. Let's proceed to the meaty part where you run this as a Pod in K8s.

Start creating YAML for it. The YAML can be found at https://github. com/prateek2408/BookExamples/tree/main/gRPC/pod.yaml.

Before creating a Pod, the first thing you should do is have a dry run. A dry run is a process that simulates the entire flow of creating an object. This is done to ensure that there are no problems in the YAML. It's a good practice to do a dry run before creating an object in K8s. To perform a dry run, simply add *--dry-run=client* to the command, so it looks like this: *kubectl create --dry-run=client -f pod.yaml*.

```
$ cat pod.yaml.1
apiVersion: v1
kind: Pod
metadata:
  name: myrpc
  labels:
    app: gprc-server
spec:
  containers:
    - name: myrpc
      image: myrpc
      imagePullPolicy: IfNotPresent
      ports:
        - name: web
          containerPort: 2408
          protocol: TCP
$
$
$ kubectl create --dry-run=client -f pod.yaml.1
pod/myrpc created (dry run)
```

***Figure 2-18.** Kubectl Dry run*

Everything is standard but notice that you have set the image pull policy to **IfNotPresent**. This is because you are saying that the image for the container is present on the system, so K8s does not have to search for it in any registry (in this case, Docker Hub). If you don't change it, K8s might complain that the image is not found in the registry as this is something you created locally and won't be available in Docker Hub.

Let's run the ***kubectl create -f pod.yaml*** command and let K8s create a Pod for it. Verify the status of the Pod via **kubectl get pods myrpc.** Once it becomes Running, you can see the logs via **kubectl logs myrpc,** and they are the same as the logs you saw when you created the container manually via Docker.

```
NAME      READY    STATUS     RESTARTS    AGE
myrpc     1/1      Running    0           16s
```

Figure 2-19. *Kubernetes Pods*

You now know about Docker and Kubernetes and their respective roles and responsibilities. But the journey isn't over. The client is yet to be created. The gRPC client is poking this server on port 2408 and getting hello-world in return, so let's head to the client creation part now.

To create a client, you again use protoc. So run the Docker container and mount the path where the proto was present.

```
docker run -it --rm $PWD:/opt/ protoc bash
```

The difference here is to tell the protoc binary to generate Python libraries instead of Golang this time. The following is the command to generate Python gRPC files.

```
python3 -m grpc_tools.protoc -I.   --python_out=. --grpc_python_
out=. hello-world.proto
```

You have created many pb files, but this time with .py signifying they are Python files. Let's create a simple Python file that calls the generated client library and print what you get from the RPC as output. A sample Python client is at `https://github.com/prateek2408/BookExamples/tree/main/gRPC/client/client.py`.

Since you already know how to do the verification by now, let's create Dockerfile, which creates an image with the Python gRPC client. The Dockerfile is under the Dockerbuild-client repository. Build a docker image for the client via the following command.

```
docker build -t myrpc-client -f Dockerbuild-client
```

Since the image is built, let's host it inside K8s as a Pod. Let's create another YAML for client-Pod.

```
apiVersion: v1
kind: Pod
metadata:
  name: client
spec:
  containers:
  - name: client
    image: myrpc-client
    env:
      - name: SERVER_URL
        value: "CLUELESS"
```

Notice the SERVER_URL environment variable, which is set to CLUELESS because you are unaware of what to set here. :) Don't worry. Let's fix that part now. To fix this, let's discuss how Pods in K8s communicate. In K8s, there is something known as a service. A service is a name that you give to a Pod, and you can access that Pod via that service name from within the cluster. A Kube-DNS service is deployed in every

K8s cluster, which resolves the service name to its internal IP. For example, if your service name is Mario, it is accessible by ***Mario.svc.Kubernetes. cluster.local.*** Pretty neat, right! But there is one problem: you never created a service for the gRPC server Pod. Now that you know the service, let's create one. You need it for the use case.

```
apiVersion: v1
kind: Service
metadata:
  name: mycat-service
spec:
  selector:
    app: mycat
  ports:
    - protocol: TCP
      port: 80
      targetPort: 9376
```

This YAML creates a service in the K8s cluster for your Pod, and the way K8s maps everything is by matching labels. Notice you have given the same label that server Pod has so that K8s can match it and attach this service object to the Pod. Sounds legit, right? Let's create the service YAML via the **kubectl create -f mycat-service-svc.yaml** command. Then, run ***kubectl get svc mycat-service*** to see the status of your service. Based on the ports you gave in the Pod and SVC YAML, you see that the port 2408 on TCP is exposed, and it's the duty of K8s to route traffic coming on this SVC on port 2408 to the respective container.

If you are interested in learning more about service in K8s, head over to https://kubernetes.io/docs/concepts/services-networking/service/.

Let's go back to the CLUELESS part since you know what needs to be set there. The following is the updated YAML.

```yaml
apiVersion: v1
kind: Pod
metadata:
  name: client
spec:
  containers:
  - name: client
    image: myrpc-client
    env:
      - name: SERVER_URL
        value: "mycat-service.svc.kubernetes.cluster.local"
```

Create this Pod straightaway via the **kubectl create -f python-hello-world.yaml** command and check its status via the **kubectl get pods python-client-hello-world** command. If it's running, use the *kubectl logs python-client-hello-world* command to see the logs. It should show you the RPC response, as shown in Figure 2-20.

```
root@dummy-machine$ kubectl logs python-client-hello-world
Hey There
```

Figure 2-20. *kubectl logs*

Congratulations, you just created a gRPC server in Golang and a client in Python from scratch and hosted it on your cluster. You're a pro now!

Differences in Creating Applications for Kubernetes

So far, you have developed and deployed multiple applications on Kubernetes. If you notice the steps and process, they are more or less the same for all the applications. But that does not necessarily mean that it always be the same. Let's try to understand this by using the use-case strategy. In the previous section of this chapter, you created a Python gRPC client. The client was always running, and it was constantly poking the server at an interval of 5 seconds. It means that the client was constantly demanding to fetch the result from the server. What if the Python client needs to call the server only once? What happens then?

In K8s, every entity is considered an object. There are different kinds of objects that Kubernetes support. The Kind field in every YAML defines the type of object to be created. The Pods, Services, PV, and PVC objects are a few of the ones you have studied. Now let's dive deeper into the world of objects to see what's available and what they aim to do.

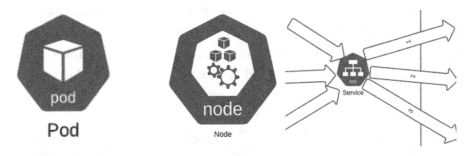

Figure 2-21. *Objects*

- **Pod**: This is the most granular one, and it can contain a bunch of containers that need to be hosted on the K8s cluster. Mostly all other objects indirectly use Pod because it sits at the heart of everything.

- **Service**: This object does not create a container but a mapping to reach another object by a name on the defined port for the specified protocol.

- **ReplicaSets**: In the older versions of K8s, a user creates ReplicationControllers to ensure that multiple duplicate Pods are running to handle failover and provide resiliency to the application. ReplicationControllers are no longer exposed to the user and are a part of deployment.

- **Deployment**: This object sits on top of a ReplicationController (RC) to create multiple RCs as defined in the YAML. RC internally creates Pods, so the concept is still the same (i.e., to provide high availability and resiliency to the applications running in the Pod).

- **PersistentVolume (PV)**: You created PV in the subchapter earlier to mount a path on the host system as a volume to the Pod.

- **PersistentVolumeClaim (PVC)**: To claim a PV, you use PVC, and whatever values you provide in the storage class field, an appropriate PV is chosen based on that.

- **Job**: This object creates a Pod with the aim that the service inside the Pod needs to run only once, like a non-recurring task.

- **CronJob**: Similar to Job but also has the Linux cron system inbuilt into it. It helps run the job whenever the user specifies it to run. Consider this when you want to schedule the running of the Pod every day or every hour.

- **ConfigMap**: All applications need a config or initialization file to start up. These files contain environment-specific things such as database details, logging level, and application-specific flags. K8s provides an in-house system to store your application configs in a ConfigMap object.

- **Secrets**: Sensitive values should be stored in an encrypted system. For this, you can use secrets. (The encryption is base64, so it's not that advanced. If the information is highly sensitive, prefer using an external vault service instead.)

- **Namespaces**: This Kubernetes object segregates all the objects created for a software stack. You can use Namespaces to create multiple environments like staging, development, and preproduction. You can use namespaces to segregate different departments. In an organization, departments can be like HR, admin, finance, and R&D, where there can be a namespace for every department. Role-based access control (RBAC) can be set up at the namespace level. It's up to you how you use it, but the core concept is to group all the similar objects in a namespace.

All the important objects are listed; it would be an endless list if I tried to write all the available objects. Remember, a Pod is the building block of K8s, so you might find a Pod inside many objects. As you know a bit about objects, let's come back to the problem statement (i.e., if you can choose a better object for our Python-based gRPC client). The engineering team has decided that the Python gRPC client needs to run only once for the Hello World application, and you need to make changes. Let's create a different kind of object to suit our requirements.

Based on your learning about objects, the most suitable one is the Job object because it runs a Pod with the intent that it's a one-time task. Let's make the changes to the Python client YAML as follows.

```
apiVersion: v1
kind: Job
metadata:
  name: client
  restarts: 2
spec:
  containers:
  - name: client
    image: myrpc-client
    env:
      - name: SERVER_URL
        value: "mycat-service.svc.kubernetes.cluster.local"
```

As you can see, the object kind has now been changed to Job. Along with that, RestartCount in the YAML specifies if K8s needs to retry running the job if the Pod that is specified in the object fails. You have set it to 6, which means if the Pod crashes during execution, K8s restarts it but only six times. After that, it marks it as failed. Also, note that there is already a Pod present, so let's delete the old one via the **kubectl delete -f python-gRPC-client.yaml** command. Finally, create a Job object via the **kubectl create -f python-gGRPC-client-job.yaml** command.

```
kubectl get jobs python-grpc-client-job
NAME                      COMPLETIONS  DURATION  AGE
python-grpc-client-job  0/1          12s       12s
```

Figure 2-22. *Job overview*

```
kubectl get pods
NAME                         READY  STATUS   RESTARTS  AGE
python-grpc-client-job-4dvtm  1/1   Running  0         2m40s
```

Figure 2-23. *Pod overview (running)*

Cool, It's all done now. Check the status via the **kubectl get jobs python-grpc-client-job** command, and you should see something similar to Figure 2-22. It's all good now because the job is in the running phase but hasn't finished yet. Remember that as a job inside creates a Pod, you see it for that respective job when you use **kubectl get pods**. But when there are many Pods in the system, how to ensure which Pod represents your job? Let's map it.

To start mapping your job with its respective Pod, you must iterate through the system like a tree by following these steps.

1.   Run the **kubectl describe pod python-grpc-client** command. Focus on the part shown in Figure 2-24.

Here, it shows the Pod attached to the job you created.

```
kubectl describe pod python-grpc-client
Name:            python-grpc-client-job-4dvtm
Namespace:   default
Priority:        0
Node:            node-pool1
Start Time:      Thu, 4 Apr 2022
Labels:          controller-uid=99141390-8ee2-4f09-b323-ad18
                 job-name=python-grpc-client-job
Annotations:   <none>
Status:          Succeeded
IP:              10.148.2.9
IPs:
 IP:             10.148.2.9
Controlled By:  Job/python-grpc-client-job
```

Figure 2-24. *Job description*

2. Run the **kubectl get pod** command and see the
    status of the Pod.

It's running, and everything is normal.

As you have found the tree and are now sure which Pod is linked to
the job, let's head over to the logs and see what the application is doing.
Run the **kubectl logs python-grpc-client-job-4dvtm** command, and you
should see something similar to Figure 2-25.

```
user@mymachine: kubectl logs python-grpc-client-job-4dvtm
Greeter client received: Hey There
Greeter client received: Hey There
Greeter client received: Hey There
Greeter client received: Hey There
Greeter client received: Hey There
Greeter client received: Hey There
Greeter client received: Hey There
Greeter client received: Hey There
Greeter client received: Hey There
Greeter client received: Hey There
Greeter client received: Hey There
Greeter client received: Hey There
```

Figure 2-25. *Pod logs*

Based on the logs, the client is trying to fetch the response repeatedly, which makes the service run endlessly. Remember that our engineering team asked us to modify the client to fetch the response only once. To achieve this, you did change the object type from Pod to Job but clearly, only doing that does not work.

If you observe the code closely, you find a loop in the logic that constantly tries to connect to the gRPC server. After connecting, it fetches the response. The loop is specifically at line 10. See `https://github.com/prateek2408/BookExamples/blob/main/gRPC/client/client.py#L10`. It would be perfectly fine to run this code inside a Pod object. But in the Job object, it is expected that the container runs to perform a specified task and then finish. In that case, the logic of the code is bad, as the process runs forever. To complete the requirements, you must do the following.

1.   Modify the client code to run once and not in a forever loop.

2.   Build the image with the updated code.

Let's modify the client code to look like the following.

```
server_addr = os.getenv("SERVER_URL")
channel = grpc.insecure_channel(server_addr)
stub = hello_world_pb2_grpc.MyServiceStub(channel)
response = stub.MyFunc(hello_world_pb2.Request())
print("Greeter client received: " + response.message)
```

You removed the while loop from the code and made the client fetch responses only once. Now build the image via the **docker build -t <IMAGE_NAME> -f Dockerfile** command.

Once the image is built, you must delete the job and create it again so that the Pod is created with the latest image you just built. Run the following commands to re-create the job with the new image.

- **kubectl delete -f PYTHON_CLIENT_JOB_gRPC.yaml**

- **kubectl create -f PYTHONH_CLIENT_JOB_ gRPC.yaml**

Okay, so that was a bit of a task. Now see the job status by running the **kubectl get jobs** command. Notice that the job status is reflected as finished, whereas the Pod is shown as completed. So now you know that the Pod was not going to last forever, and as it's a job, K8s marked it as completed.

Note   If you had not changed the code, it would not have made any sense because the job would never have finished. It's not only the object you choose in K8s, but the application also needs to support that kind of object.

As a developer and cloud systems designer, you must know which objects create which kind of applications because every object works differently. Creating a job for an application that runs 24/7 is useless, and creating a deployment for a service that should run only once a day does not make sense. Your duty is to architect the services running on your cluster to align everything. Based on the nature of the application and requirement, appropriate objects are created in K8s.

When an application runs, you always consider what happens if it crashes? Crashing of applications is inevitable, and restarting applications is bound to happen. Developers always have the state of the application maintained in some or the other way. It can be as simple as having a flat file that the application reads and understands what it is doing, or it can be a database. In K8s, you host all applications in a Pod, which opens another question for discussion: What is the state of a Pod? When the application Pod restarts, does it get the same Pod?

State of a Pod

By default, a Pod and the containers inside the Pod are stateless. This means they can restart, crash, and don't have any state attached to them. Further, when a Pod is restarted, it gets created with the same image, but the container ID and IP are changed. Even the connections it makes to other services are all new. So if you are in the process of deploying a stateful application that has the mechanism of running multiple instances of it in a cluster and each instance has a state associated with it, keep in mind that things like hostname and IP play a vital role in it. To solve scenarios where an application running inside a Pod needs a state, the StatefulSets object ensures that the Pods that get created have a static hostname and their IPs don't change in restarts.

The StatefulSets object also provides an identity to the Pod. The identity sticks to the Pod, regardless of which node it's (re)scheduled on. A good example of a StatefulSets object is when you run database software systems in high availability (HA) mode on Kubernetes. Let's look at a MySQL database, where you want to create multiple replicas of the database to make it run in an HA fashion. Since it's a database, when you access it, you want one primary node/replica to provide the output and all other replicas to sync the data between them. You can achieve this by using the StatefulSets object.

First, let's do this without the StatefulSets object to see how it looks. Figure 2-26 illustrates a MySQL cluster deployed without it.

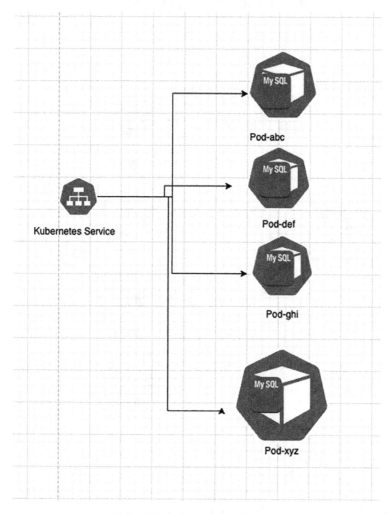

Figure 2-26. *MySQL in Kubernetes*

This creates a MySQL deployment and a service to access the deployment. Finally, you increased the replicas to four since you want the database to run in HA mode. For the application to work in a clustered fashion, every instance should be able to uniquely identify the other instances. This is not possible in this case because if Pod-abc dies, it is re-created with a different random ID, say Pod-jkl. So, this kind of deployment won't work. Let's re-create the MySQL deployment with StatefulSets deployed, as illustrated in Figure 2-27.

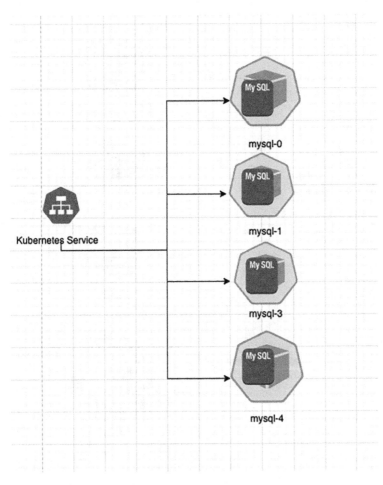

Figure 2-27. *MySQL in Kubernetes (StatefulSets)*

The notable difference you see is that now every Pod comes with its own unique identity, which never changes. Even during a Pod restart, say mysql-0, the hostname never changes. This feature of Kubernetes makes the deployment of applications like MySQL possible as now they can run in a clustered fashion. You might be thinking that in this case, the database is still inside the Pod and although after a restart, the ID is persisted. What about the data? You can add persistent volumes as well and have a 1-0-1 mapping with the Pod. Figure 2-28 illustrates this where you add PVs to the Pods.

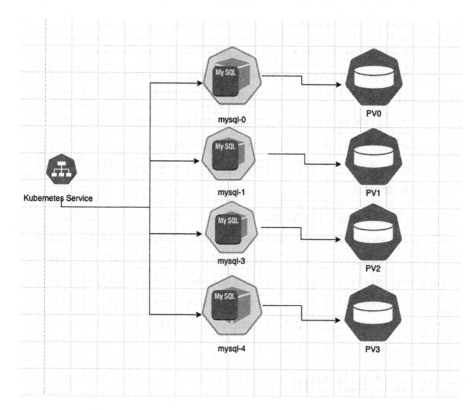

Figure 2-28. *MySQL in Kubernetes (StatefulSets, PVs)*

On that note, here are a few key takeaways.

- If there are multiple microservices to be hosted on K8s, then identify the nature of each microservice, where they should be placed in K8s, and under which object.

- If there is only one fat binary that does everything, K8s probably might not solve your use case. In the transition phase, consider creating a low-level design (LLD) or high-level design (HLD) to transform the monolithic application into microservices to leverage K8s and its potential.

- In production-grade services, microservices are always deployed as a Deployment object, which creates replicas and acts as a manager for the Pods.

- The application needs to blend with the system to leverage its full potential. Developing applications should always be done keeping the system behavior in mind.

An application running in the cluster need to be accessed by the outside world so that the end users can leverage its use. Imagine running thousands of Pods in your K8s cluster, but no one can access it, or there is no way built in the system to enable a user to reach it. This makes the entire solution useless. It is very important to discuss how Kubernetes enables access to the application for their end users.

Ingress Controller

As you progress towards learning, creating services, and knowing objects available in K8s, you are getting confident with the system and attaining decent knowledge about how things work. There is still a crucial case uncovered in your journey: access. As a developer, you can do the following.

1. Develop your microservice.

2. Build a docker image.

3. Deploy in your development K8s cluster.

4. Run/Test it by accessing the application using the port-forward utility.

5. Push the application image to some public/private registry.

Your work as a developer is done.

Now let me ask you a question. In an actual scenario where there is a web UI hosted on the K8s cluster, how can it be accessed from the public world via a browser? You're puzzled, right?

There is a piece that I haven't covered yet: ingress controllers. An ingress controller is a service where all the incoming traffic land. Once it lands, traffic is forwarded to the respective application based on rules.

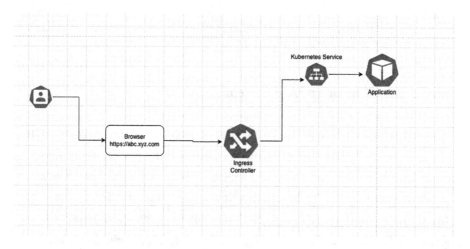

Figure 2-29. *Ingress controller*

Sounds simple, right? Let's head over and create an ingress controller. Let's stick to the Nginx ingress controller, which is popular and widely used in this case.

Installation Steps

The ingress controller routes traffic on a domain basis. When an ingress controller comes up, it binds itself to a domain, say *.mario.com*, where **mario.com** is a domain, and you are its owner. The * in the field is a wildcard that denotes the entire subdomain. This wildcard (*) is the playground of the ingress controller. So, if a request comes to **app1.mario. com**, the ingress controller takes care of it. First, it checks if there are rules for this address configured. If found, it forwards the traffic to the service configured for **app1.mario.com**; otherwise, it returns a 404 NOT FOUND error. Figure 2-30 illustrates the flow.

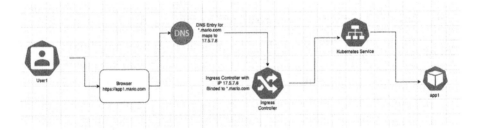

Figure 2-30. *Flow of app1.mario.com*

Let's proceed with installing an ingress controller on your cluster. This exercise uses the Nginx ingress controller, but if you work on a managed version of Kubernetes such as GKE, AKS, and EKS, you can choose any other ingress controller. To install the Nginx ingress controller, run the **kubectl apply -f https://raw.githubusercontent.com/kubernetes/ ingress-nginx/controller-v1.1.3/deploy/static/provider/cloud/ deploy.yaml** command. If you are running everything on minikube, enabling ingress is as easy as running the **minikube addons enable ingress** command. Configuring and bringing an ingress controller can be tricky as it broadly involves the following items.

1. Install the ingress controller (the easy part).

2. Expose the Controller service object to a public IP (service type is load balancer).

3. Configure the controller to bind to a domain (for example, *.mario.com).

4. Configure the DNS provider to add an entry that maps the domain to the public IP of the controller (i.e., *.mario.com to 17.5.7.8).

Once these following steps are done, your ingress controller should be up and running and ready to be used for routing external traffic to applications running on the cluster. If you are struggling with bringing up an ingress controller, I suggest you stick to minikube since it's easy.

Access an Application via Ingress Controller

After installation, based on your K8s flavor, you get the URL on which the ingress controller is listening.

Since the ingress controller is up and running as a Pod, let's see if you can create some rules and reach the application deployed in the cluster. Remember you created an Apache server? Let's use it here. If you deleted the Pod, don't worry; you can make a new one following the same steps.

Considering that your Apache server is running, let's create a service for it first via the following YAML.

```
apiVersion: v1
kind: Service
metadata:
```

```
  name: apache-svc
spec:
  selector:
    app: apache
  ports:
    - protocol: TCP
      port: 8080
      targetPort: 8080
```

Create the service via the **kubectl create -f apache-svc.yaml** command. Proceed with creating ingress rules. The following is the YAML for it.

```
apiVersion: networking.k8s.io/v1
kind: Ingress
metadata:
  name: apache
  annotations:
    nginx.ingress.kubernetes.io/rewrite-target: /
spec:
  ingressClassName: nginx-example
  rules:
  - http:
      paths:
      - path: /
        pathType: Prefix
        backend:
          service:
            name: apache-svc
            port:
              number: 8080
```

Note that in the YAML, an ingress is an object (in K8s, everything is an object). Once this is created, the ingress controller is told that whatever traffic is coming for domain **apache.mario.com** should be routed to the apache service. That's it. You are all good to go. The ingress controller constantly looks for updates and updates itself with the rules. Head over to your browser and type **http://apache.mario.com.**

Note   You might get a warning as SSL certificates are self-signed. In an actual scenario, the certs are signed by a known authority, so this warning does not come.

Apache2 Debian Default Page

debian

It works!

This is the default welcome page used to test the correct operation of the Apache2 server after installation on Debian systems. If you can read this page, it means that the Apache HTTP server installed at this site is working properly. You should **replace this file** (located at /var/www /html/index.html) before continuing to operate your HTTP server.

If you are a normal user of this web site and don't know what this page is about, this probably means that the site is currently unavailable due to maintenance. If the problem persists, please contact the site's administrator.

Configuration Overview

Debian's Apache2 default configuration is different from the upstream default configuration, and split into several files optimized for interaction with Debian tools. The configuration system is **fully documented in /usr/share/doc/apache2/README.Debian.gz**. Refer to this for the full documentation. Documentation for the web server itself can be found by accessing the **manual** if the apache2-doc package was installed on this server.

The configuration layout for an Apache2 web server installation on Debian systems is as follows:

```
/etc/apache2/
|-- apache2.conf
|       `-- ports.conf
|-- mods-enabled
|       |-- *.load
|       `-- *.conf
|-- conf-enabled
|       `-- *.conf
|-- sites-enabled
|       `-- *.conf
```

- apache2.conf is the main configuration file. It puts the pieces together by including all remaining configuration files when starting up the web server.

- ports.conf is always included from the main configuration file. It is used to determine the listening ports for incoming connections, and this file can be customized anytime.

- Configuration files in the mods-enabled/, conf-enabled/ and sites-enabled/ directories contain particular configuration snippets which manage modules, global configuration fragments, or virtual host configurations, respectively.

- They are activated by symlinking available configuration files from their respective *-available/ counterparts. These should be managed by using our helpers a2enmod, a2dismod, a2ensite, a2dissite, and a2enconf, a2disconf . See their respective man pages for detailed information.

- The binary is called apache2. Due to the use of environment variables, in the default configuration, apache2 needs to be started/stopped with /etc/init.d/apache2 or apache2ctl. **Calling /usr/bin/apache2 directly will not work** with the default configuration.

Document Roots

By default, Debian does not allow access through the web browser to *any* file apart of those located in /var/www, **public_html** directories (when enabled) and /usr/share (for web applications). If your site is using a web document root located elsewhere (such as in /srv) you may need to whitelist your document root directory in /etc/apache2/apache2.conf.

The default Debian document root is /var/www/html. You can make your own virtual hosts under /var/www. This is different to previous releases which provides better security out of the box.

Reporting Problems

Please use the reportbug tool to report bugs in the Apache2 package with Debian. However, check **existing bug reports** before reporting a new bug.

Please report bugs specific to modules (such as PHP and others) to respective packages, not to the web server itself.

Figure 2-31. *Apache server via ingress controller*

Hurray, your application's traffic is routing from the ingress controller to the Pod. Isn't it cool? It is now perfectly appropriate to say that the ingress controller (Nginx) acts as the reverse proxy agent. It is waiting to get traffic for all the configured microservices in the cluster. It is the gateway that handles all the incoming traffic.

Summary

This chapter was all about developing applications for the Kubernetes cluster. You learned how to start everything from scratch, how to mount volumes, where to create jobs, and where deployments are needed. It explained ingress controllers, demonstrated how applications are accessed in production-grade systems, and created ingress rules for your application running on K8s.

This journey has missed a significant part of the software life cycle: testing. We tend to neglect it, but it is proven that every time a feature or code is added to the software, a bug is injected. If there is a proper testing system for the application, and the code coverage is above 85%, then finding runtime bugs in software is drastically reduced. The reasons you neglect are due to the following.

- It is repetitive.

- It is boring to write test cases.

- It takes time, and the code must be merged as soon as possible.

- It is manual and tiring.

The reasons can be endless and vary on the nature of the work and project. But let's face it, testing is necessary and should be part of the software development life cycle (SDLC). I covered testing to help you understand that an engineer should never neglect testing. Since testing is a topic itself, it isn't covered in this book. However, frameworks like PyTest are used in the following chapters to show how unit testing can be integrated into the CI (continuous integration) pipelines ensuring everything is tested before being pushed.

CHAPTER 3

CI/CD Systems

Before moving to CI/CD, let's summarize what you have learned so far. You started with the basics of cloud computing—what it is and how it connects to Kubernetes. You also got to know how a Kubernetes cluster works and how to interact with it. You've gained an understanding of containerization, Docker, and images, and you know how to package a software solution and run it on a Kubernetes cluster.

In the previous chapter, you executed every step manually, from packaging the application (in images) to running them on a K8s cluster. This was intentional to help you better understand how things are done. It is now important to learn the role of automation. Automation is the key to managing, running, and scaling large and complex systems. Imagine a situation when there are two hundred applications. As an engineer, you are given a task to update the image of all the workloads running on a Kubernetes cluster. It would take you at least a day on average to complete this task manually. There can be millions of workloads in an actual world. It becomes impossible to manage such systems without automation. CI/CD (continuous integration/continuous deployment) is a culture or method that defines a set of practices that enables applications to be continuously built, deployed, and updated. Automation is the heart of any CI/CD methodology. Every step in the process is performed via a tool or an automated script, making automation the soul of CI/CD.

© Prateek Khushalani 2022
P. Khushalani, *Kubernetes Application Developer*,
https://doi.org/10.1007/978-1-4842-8032-4_3

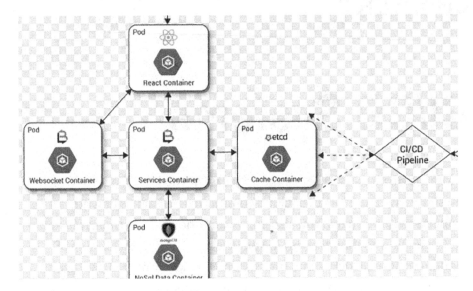

Figure 3-1. *CI/CD systems*

Overview

Traditionally, IT (information technology) teams consisted of developers and operators. Developers were responsible for writing code for systems, and operators ensured that those systems operated reliably. However, operators were isolated from the developer vertical, which often resulted in the famous issue of the developer saying, "It works on my machine." Now you have moved to an era where every software solution is eventually a collection of services, and each service is responsible for a particular task. This kind of architecture is known as microservice architecture. Every service is independent and isolated, and interaction with each service happens via an interface that can be REST, gRPC, xmlRPC, and so on.

There is a development team for every service, and the code is generally hosted on centralized locations, such as GitHub, GitLab, or Bitbucket. GIT has become the best source code keeper, and it powers all hosting solutions. In addition, every team adopts an agile business model where a collection of tasks is registered and displayed on Kanban boards.

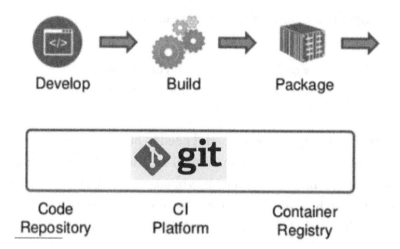

Figure 3-2. *Continuous build*

Allocation of work to developers is done in the form of tickets. All the bug fixes, features, and documentation are done as part of the ticket assigned to the developer. The developer's journey starts with the ticket, and they are expected to make necessary code changes against the ticket to complete it. Afterward, the fix for the ticket goes into the feature branch, where it is ready to be merged. But there are the following steps still left.

1. Complete testing the software, which was modified due to code changes.

2. Ensure that code quality is not degraded via code coverage, linting, and proper comments.

3. Perform unit/functional testing.

4. Merge the feature branch to the staging branch.

5. Package the software and publish it at a centralized location.

6. Update the software running in different environments.

7. Use canary builds and blue-green deployment techniques to achieve no downtime, and revert in the event of a failure.

So, you can see that many tasks still need to be done after development, and they are the same for all the fixes/enhancements going in the software branch. To do such tasks in an automated fashion, CI/CD comes to the aid. But before you deep dive into what CI/CD is and how it is achieved, let's see what the system looks like without it.

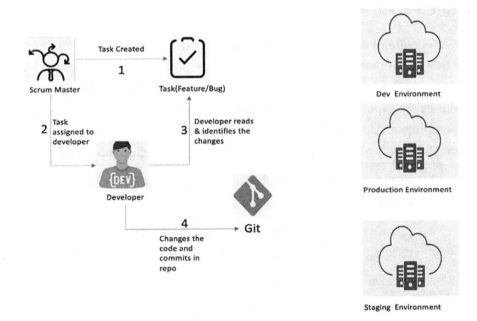

Figure 3-3. *Developer journey*

In Figure 3-3, you can see that a proper flow and process are being followed where the scrum master creates a task and assigns it to the developer. The developer then goes through the task, identifies the changes, and finally commits the code changes in the Git repo. But after that, there is a void as testing, quality, and deployment to different environments are still unknown. To fill this specific void, CI/CD comes into the picture.

CI stands for *continuous integration*, and CD stands for *continuous deployment*. The names describe perfectly what each is doing. CI has jobs consisting of unit/module/functional testing, code coverage, linting, and CD run after CI and do the packaging, deployment, and upgrading of the software running in different environments. A rich collection of CI/CD systems is available in the market, such as Jenkins, Travis, Concourse, GitLab, or GitHub Actions.

No matter which CI you choose, always remember that at the core level, every solution runs jobs/tasks/pipelines that aim to test, build, package, and ship the software solution for which they are made. Figure 3-4 shows the complete picture.

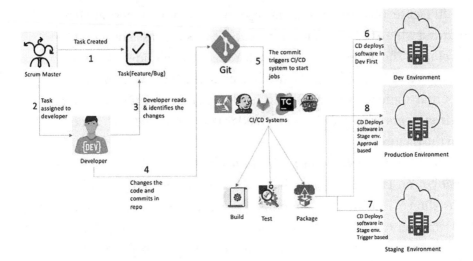

Figure 3-4. *Developer's journey with CI/CD*

CI/CD systems offer win-win scenarios.

- Developers are happy because they can focus on their core work and add more value.

- Managers and scrum masters are delighted because they have a dashboard to see everything in action.

- Customers are satisfied because the turnaround time to get features in production is reduced. Everything is automated and done with a button click without any downtime.

Under the Hood

Let's now drill down into each component separately to understand its role and know how every component differs.

Continuous Integration (CI)

Continuous integration is the practice where developers merge changes to the code base to the feature branch, also known as trunk or main. The frequency can be dynamic based on the load. It can inject 20 to 200 features in a single day. Typically, in a sprint model, when the sprint is nearing completion, you see a lot of merges happening in a single day. These changes are validated by creating a build and running automated tests against the build. If these tests don't pass, the changes aren't merged, and developers work on providing their fixes to the issues reported. A typical example is where developers' code change reduces the total code coverage. Figure 3-5 shows how it looks if you focus on CI.

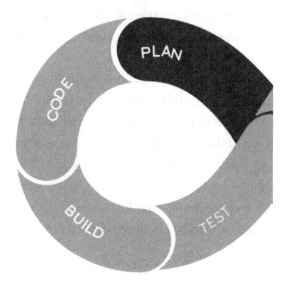

Figure 3-5. *CI cycle overview*

CI is a circular process and is best represented via a cycle. The process is bound to end when the test cases are a success, and the report generated by the CI system is acceptable. This process is generic and is domain and language agnostic. Whether you are doing development for a web application or a system-level application, the process remains the same no matter which programming language you prefer to use. This process also causes fewer bugs to be shipped to production as the issues are caught early, and integration issues are solved before release.

Continuous Delivery (CD)

Continuous delivery is an extension of CI, as it enables automation to deploy all the code changes to an environment (dev, QA, stage, prod, etc.) after the changes have been merged. Typically the main branch or trunk is not directly packaged and deployed in a production environment. No matter how lean your application ecosystem is, there is still at least one environment where the changes are staged. The staging environment is seen as a demo environment that reviews the changes before moving to production.

The artifact or the packaged binary of the application may be built as part of CI or the process. Even if it comes from the CI pipeline, the source of truth (your repository) is reliable. In simple terms, there is an automated release process on top of the automated testing process. Developers can deploy their changes by simply clicking a button or after the completion of CI. Now you might be confused. What is the difference between continuous delivery and continuous deployment? Don't worry! This is covered after you learn continuous deployment. Figure 3-6 illustrates continuous delivery.

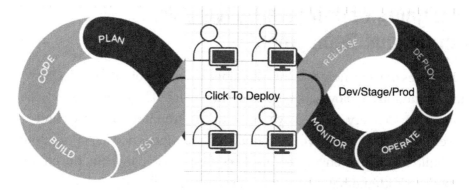

Figure 3-6. *Continuous delivery*

Continuous Deployment (CD)

Continuous deployment takes the process one step further than continuous delivery. Here, all changes that pass the verification steps at each stage in the pipeline are released to production. This process is entirely automated, and only a failed verification step prevents pushing the changes to production. Figure 3-7 is an overview.

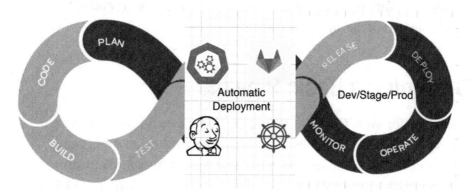

Figure 3-7. *Continuous deployment*

Designing Continuous Delivery vs. Continuous Deployment

It becomes obvious now that the difference between continuous delivery and continuous deployment lies in how deployment happens. In continuous delivery, the deployment to the environment is manual and governed by developers, where manual intervention is needed to promote the build to different environments. In continuous deployment, the entire deployment is automated and done mostly via tools.

As a best practice, it is recommended to adopt a dynamic approach where both techniques can be used based on the particular use case.

For example, a CI stage should be complemented by a continuous delivery stage where developers can promote deployments and upgrade to different environments such as non-production, staging, or sandbox. However, keep in mind not to provide the developers a way to promote deployment to a prod environment. Finally, continuous deployment, an automated process, should be used in production environments. Automatic checks and intelligent deployment techniques such as canary deployment with rollback based on automated monitoring and KPIs should be part of this deployment.

Designing a Basic Pipeline

The basics for every CI/CD are the same. CI focuses on code building, testing, and quality. CD focuses on packaging, pushing to a repo, and refreshing the environments with the newer versions of the software.

Every task can be called a job at a granular level, and many jobs form a pipeline. You might hear something like "the pipeline has failed" on Jenkins, GitLab, Travis, or whatever software solution your team uses for CI/CD. Generally, a DevOps engineer investigates the pipeline failure, does some magic, and it starts working again. In a fault in the code commit, the developer needs to fix the code changes that caused a job in the pipeline to fail.

What do these jobs look like, and how do you create them? Let's build a sample job for Python software in the Travis system.

Let's use an application written in Python and stored on GitHub. The application generates tiny URLs. It's a simple application but does not have any CI system. You want to create a job that tests the application using the PyTest framework. The repository is at `https://github.com/` `prateek2408/magicurl`.

Creating a CI System for Testing

Let's create a CI for the same project hosted on GitHub. First, create a repository in GitHub and name it whatever you like. In this scenario, the repository's name is magicurl; it is hosted at `https://github.com/` `prateek2408/magicurl`. It contains a Python application that generates a short URL for all the lengthy URLs that it receives in the request payload. This exercise won't go deeper into how the application works because that is not the intent. The CI/CD solution used for the application is Travis. Travis can be easily integrated with GitHub repos, and it's free, so you don't need to pay for it. For extensive cases where your organization needs custom hardware to run jobs, TravisPro provides custom deployments of a proprietary version on the customer's hardware.

You need to log in to Travis and sign in with GitHub to integrate your project. Then, navigate to Settings under your profile, and click the **Sync account** button, as seen in Figure 3-8.

Figure 3-8. *Travis UI*

Under the Repository section, you should see all your GitHub repositories linked to your account; by default, all the repositories are disabled, which means Travis is not enabled for them. In this example, you use the **magicurl** repository. Turn it on by toggling the slider. Whatever repo you are integrating with, make sure to enable its integration with Travis also.

Next, hit the Settings link on the right side of the repo you have enabled, which takes you to the Settings page. From here, you can configure it as follows.

1. Run CI for all the branches in the repository.

2. Run CI for all the PRs that are created in the repository.

3. Set a limit to the number of concurrent jobs that can be created.

4. Run CI only on the branch's latest commit and cancel CI jobs on the old commit.

5. Set environment variables.

    a. All application-specific variables can be exported here.

    b. The credentials can be kept here if your app needs to be pushed to Artifactory or Docker Hub as a docker image.

6. Handle beta features.

A simple Pylint job is run for this Python application, so let's keep the settings as they are. If you click the dashboard on the Travis UI, you should see something like Figure 3-9.

Figure 3-9. *Repositories in Travis UI*

This image tells that your repo hosted on GitHub is not integrated with Travis and is ready for creating jobs and a CI pipeline. If you click **Trigger a build,** nothing happens; the YAML, which tells Travis about the jobs, is not present in the repository. Let's create a basic Travis YAML that does flake testing on a Python application.

```
==========================
language: python
python: 3.8

install:
  - pip -r requirements.txt
scripts:
  - pytest --flake8
==========================
```

Add this file as **.travis.yml** in your GitHub repo.

Let's look at the operations the file is performing.

- **language**: This tells Travis which language the job should run. Since this application (**magicurl**) is Python-based, Python is the value.

- **version**: Travis YAML gives an option to provide the language version. This example uses Python version 3.8.

- **install**: Before running the actual job, there might be some dependencies that you need to install. To do that, you have this section. In this case, you need all the modules defined in **requirements.txt** to be installed before the flake testing.

- **scripts**: In this section, you write what the job runs or tests. You want to run the flake test cases, so you have the relevant command in that section.

There is a catch. You have knowingly injected an error in the **pip** command. Error is injected to check and identify the flow of what Travis is doing. Add this to your repo and then commit or hover to the dashboard and manually trigger a build. In this case, the build fails, giving the error about the **pip** command, as shown in Figure 3-10.

```
$ source ~/virtualenv/python3.8/bin/activate
$ python --version
Python 3.8.7
$ pip --version
pip 20.3.3 from /home/travis/virtualenv/python3.8.7/lib/python3.8/site-packages/pip (python 3.8)
$ pip -r requirements.txt

Usage:
  pip <command> [options]

no such option: -r
The command "pip -r requirements.txt" failed and exited with 2 during .

Your build has been stopped.
```

Figure 3-10. *Build overview*

Let's quickly fix the injected issue and let the CI pass. To fix this, you correct the pip command from **pip -r requirements.txt** to **pip install -r requirements.txt**. The correct Travis file is at `https://github.com/prateek2408/magicurl/blob/main/.travis.yml`.

Once you update your Travis file, the build starts automatically against the commit. Congratulations, you have now created a CI job for your project in Travis. Even if the CI solution changes to Jenkins, GitLab, or Concourse, remember the concepts remain the same. At a conceptual level, every CI's job is to read the config and run all the jobs present in the config.

Figure 3-11 shows what a commit in Travis contains.

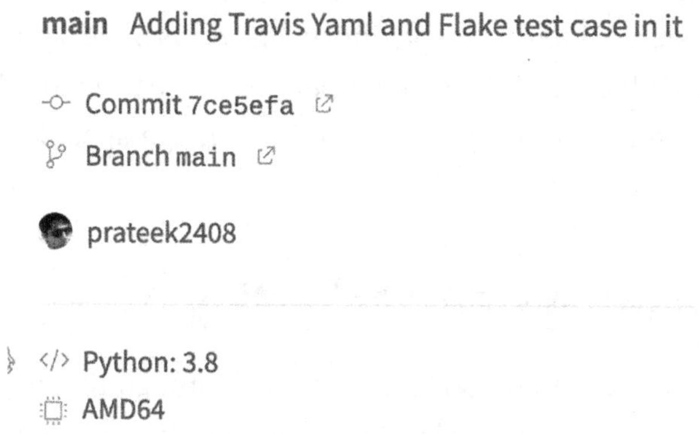

main Adding Travis Yaml and Flake test case in it

-○- Commit 7ce5efa ⬀

⅄ Branch main ⬀

● prateek2408

⅄ </> Python: 3.8

⌶ AMD64

Figure 3-11. *Commit overview, which caused the failure*

The Commit view is helpful; it includes the following.

- The Commit ID tells who committed to the repository and the changes that were checked in

- The environment in which the job is running

- The branch for which the job is running

Application-Specific CI

Though the process of the CI is language agnostic, it's always good to remember what tools to use for the language in which the application is developed for creating its respective CI. Always use the specific language's recommended tools for testing the application and make sure the pipeline is as lean and informative as possible.

The pipelines should be made so that they are modular, and new functionalities and changes can be incorporated quickly. For example, you often make a pipeline based on the nature of the application, which makes the pipeline application-centric and less modular. The best practice is to create a pipeline based on the programming language and not the application. Also, use language-specific testing tools in designing such pipelines. As an advantage, the same pipeline can be used in other similar applications because the pipeline created is language-specific and not application-centric.

Creating a CD System for Testing

Similar to what you did for making a continuous integration pipeline, let's add a continuous deployment pipeline by taking what is built in the CI step and deploying it to an environment. In this case, a sample application known as **magicurl** goes through a flake testing job before adding a new commit. Since it was just for demonstration purposes, it only consisted of one job but ideally also has the build stage. Once the testing is successfully done, an artifact is built. The nature of the artifact varies from what's the end goal and how you package your software.

Creating a docker image makes sense since the focus is on containerization and running everything on a Kubernetes cluster. Once the docker image is built, you can host it in a Docker container registry. Recall that registries act as a storehouse of container images. For this scenario, you use the Docker Hub registry for hosting the image. The Dockerfile helps create a docker image for the magicurl application (see `https://github.com/prateek2408/magicurl/blob/main/Dockerfile`).

You have selected the application for which you create the CD pipeline and have the Dockerfile to create the image. Now let's start by creating a simple pipeline that does the build. Use Travis to build the docker image. Start by editing the **.travis.yml** file.

```
services:
  - docker

before_install:
  - docker build -t prateek2408/magicurl
- docker push prateek2408/magicurl.
```

In the YAML, you provide a way for Travis to build the docker image and push it to the Docker Hub registry. When it comes it pushing images, the step fails because you haven't provided the credentials. So make sure you add a command similar to echo "$DOCKER_PASSWORD" | docker login -u "$DOCKER_USERNAME" --password-stdin.

The next time the CI runs, it runs the flake test, and once it passes, it builds and pushes the docker image. Once the image is pushed, anyone can pull it. You can see the page at `https://hub.docker.com/repository/docker/prateek2408/magicurl/general`.

Adding a Simple CD System Stage

Let's make another CI but this time, use Jenkins, where you set up Jenkins on your local environments. Then use the RBAC plugin to make sure only users assigned the role can trigger the CI job. To set up Jenkins, run the following command on your machine.

```
docker run -it --rm -p 8080:8080 jenkins/jenkins
```

This command takes up the terminal as the container is not running as a daemon process. Also, please note to copy the administrator password that comes on the terminal, as shown in Figure 3-12.

Figure 3-12. *Jenkins startup logs*

In your browser, navigate to `http://localhost:8080/`. You should see the Jenkins page asking for the administrator password. Use the password you copied in the preceding step, and then move to the next page and click **Installed Suggested Plugins**. This step depends upon your Internet connection, so it may take a while as it downloads all the required plugins for Jenkins to work properly. Once it's done, you should see a screen like the one shown in Figure 3-13.

Create First Admin User

Username:

Password:

Confirm password:

Full name:

E-mail address:

Figure 3-13. *User setup in Jenkins*

Fill out the form and create a user. You created a user named *test* and a password named *test*. Continue with the next steps. Once complete, you should see the Jenkins home page, which indicates that your local Jenkins setup is up and running. For RBAC, you use the role strategy plugin (`https://plugins.jenkins.io/role-strategy/`). To install the plugin, go to Settings and open the plugin manager. Click the Available tab and search for *role*. This should give you a list of matching plugins. Select the Role-based Authorization Strategy plugin, as shown in Figure 3-14.

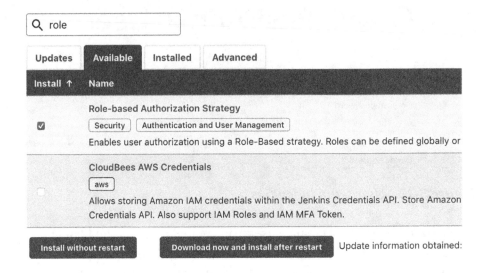

Figure 3-14. *Plugin manager in Jenkins*

Click the Install button without restarting to install the plugin on your Jenkins server. Once everything is working, click the Restart button. You should see the Jenkins home page, which asks for your username and password. Provide the credentials created in the initial steps and log in to the Jenkins server. To enable the plugin, go to the global security settings on the plugin you just installed, as shown in Figure 3-15.

Authorization

○ Anyone can do anything

○ Legacy mode

○ Logged-in users can do anything

○ Matrix-based security

○ Project-based Matrix Authorization Strategy

◉ Role-Based Strategy

Markup Formatter

Markup Formatter

> Plain text

Treats all input as plain text. HTML unsafe characters like < and

Agents

[Save]   [Apply]

Figure 3-15. *RBAC system in Jenkins*

Hit the Save button. You should then see a new option, Manage and Assign Roles, under Settings ➤ Security. Let's create some roles by going to Manage Roles. There should be four roles, with each role having build, cancel, create, or delete permission only. Once you create the role, you should see something similar to Figure 3-16.

Global roles

Role	Overall				Credentials			Agent							Job					
	Administer	Read	Create	Delete	ManageDomains	Update	View	Build	Configure	Connect	Create	Delete	Disconnect	Provision	Build	Cancel	Configure	Create	Delete	Discover
admin	☑	☑	☑	☑	☑	☑	☑	☑	☑	☑	☑	☑	☑	☑	☑	☑	☑	☑	☑	☑
role1														☑						
role2																☑				
role3																		☑		
role4														☑						

Figure 3-16. *Assigning roles to users in Jenkins*

Now proceed to the assign roles option and assign each user one of the roles you created in the preceding step. The users are not present, so once you hit Save, you might get a red cross icon on the user. This is not an issue because this warning goes away once you create the users. Figure 3-17 shows assigning roles.

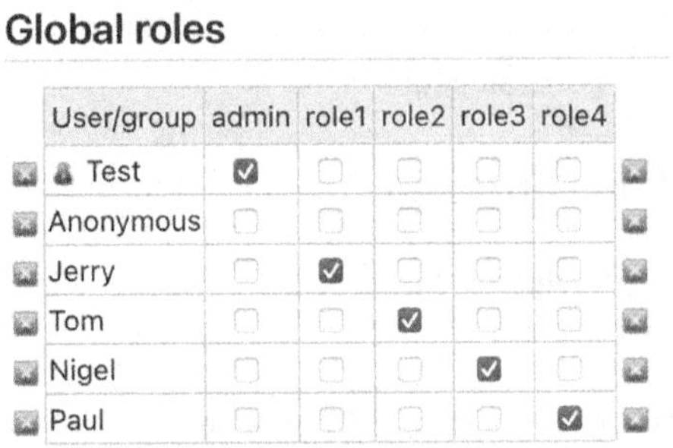

Global roles

User/group	admin	role1	role2	role3	role4	
⚫ 👤 Test	☑	☐	☐	☐	☐	☒
⚫ Anonymous	☐	☐	☐	☐	☐	☒
⚫ Jerry	☐	☑	☐	☐	☐	☒
⚫ Tom	☐	☐	☑	☐	☐	☒
⚫ Nigel	☐	☐	☐	☑	☐	☒
⚫ Paul	☐	☐	☐	☐	☑	☒

Figure 3-17. *user vs role matrix*

Finally, let's create the users. Navigate to Users under Settings and click the **Create user** button. Use the same user details you used when assigning roles in the preceding step. If the name does not match, you might face some errors in the later phase; cross-check that the names of the users match. Once everything is done, you should see something similar to Figure 3-18. Chose whatever user names and credentials you want.

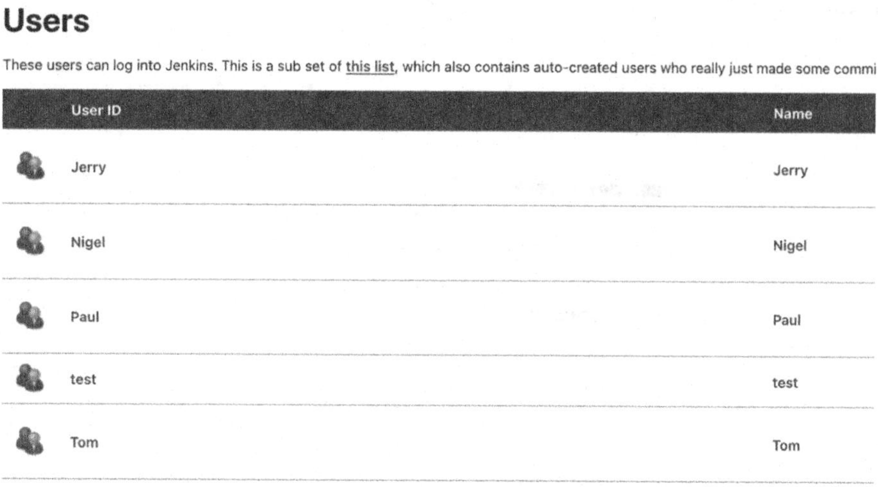

Users

These users can log into Jenkins. This is a sub set of <u>this list</u>, which also contains auto-created users who really just made some commi

	User ID	Name
🧑	Jerry	Jerry
🧑	Nigel	Nigel
🧑	Paul	Paul
🧑	test	test
🧑	Tom	Tom

Figure 3-18. *Users Overview*

Let's also configure Jenkins with a source code repository, enabling Jenkins to run pipelines whenever a commit is pushed to a branch. This makes Jenkins behave very similar to Travis, which was explored earlier. Head over to the Jenkins dashboard and create a freestyle project. Give your project a name like **my-jenkins-pipeline**. Once inside the project, head over to the settings. You should see something similar to Figure 3-19.

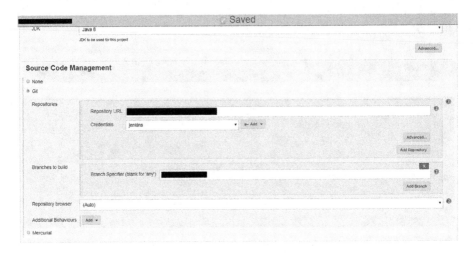

Figure 3-19. *Source code management in Jenkins*

Select Git as the source code and provide the URL (`https://github. com/prateek2408/magicurl`). In the Credentials filed, provide the username and ApiKey, which Jenkins uses for authentication. Specify the branch that you need to bind the pipeline to. If you leave this box blank, the pipeline runs on all branches.

These are a few ways you can use CI/CD systems.

Summary

Overall it is good to say that you have a fair idea about CI/CD practices and methodology. You also know the popular tools that can be leveraged to create a CI/CD system and make it a part of the software development life cycle. Following the best practices discussed when creating and designing CI/CD pipelines is always recommended. The more generic a pipeline is, the more it can scale and be applied to many like-minded applications.

With these concepts in mind, it's time to move one step further and discuss infrastructure as code. In the previous chapters, you did everything manually, including creating Kubernetes clusters, building images, and deploying applications. It was done manually to provide an in-depth understanding. Going further, you do everything via a templating and tooling system. You declare what is needed, and the tool ensures that the objects are created.

Let's go to the next chapter.

CHAPTER 4

Infrastructure as Code and Service Mesh

You have gotten your hands dirty learning how to run different applications on Kubernetes and manage automated deployment via CI/CD systems. You also went through other Kubernetes objects and learned how to mount volumes to provide persistent storage to applications running inside Pods or containers. In other words, you have a basic understanding of working on Kubernetes and if you are given an application, you can migrate/shift it to a K8s environment. If you are not confident in these areas, please pause and revise the previous chapters and topics.

Why do you need to know infrastructure as code (IaC)? Which block of the puzzle does IaC fit in? In cloud computing, one very different thing from traditional computing is how you provision your infrastructure. In the infrastructure as a service (IaaS) offering, a user provides virtual machines on which the applications run. This is very different from traditional computing since the user has contacted the infrastructure team to allocate a server for the application to run.

Provisioning of infrastructure in the cloud is now in the hands of the engineering team. This applies to all kinds of offerings that are there in the cloud. For example, even if, as a user, you want to attach a disk to your virtual machine, you have to provision it on the cloud via interfaces such

© Prateek Khushalani 2022
P. Khushalani, *Kubernetes Application Developer*,
https://doi.org/10.1007/978-1-4842-8032-4_4

as a console or command-line interface (CLI) and then finally connect it to the virtual machine. IaC does precisely this where it enables you to create and manage infrastructure on the cloud via a piece of code.

Overview

As you move along in your journey to understand the nuts and bolts of cloud and Kubernetes, there is one thing that you have frequently relied on or are dependent on, which is CLI-based tools. You have relied on many CLIs for our operations, including kubectl, docker, gcloud, and standard Linux commands. This is a good practice, and there is no problem in using CLI for performing tasks but imagine that you must perform the following tasks.

- Deploy three identical Kubernetes clusters: environments A, B, and C.

- While deploying applications on each Kubernetes environment, you need to change the image name.

If you do this via CLI, you must write the same commands for different environments. Imagine that after deploying everything, your management asks you to change the name of one of the resources in environment A. Changing the name is not possible because the dependency is tree-based. There might be a case where you have to delete the child resources to rename the parent resource.

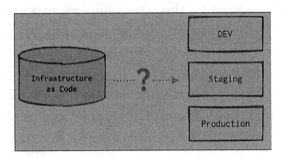

Figure 4-1. *Overview*

With this example, you quickly realize that the main problem is scalability and management. When you want to scale your solution to multiple environments or if you want to change attributes of resources, then doing it via CLI can be complicated. It is also less organized, and the dependency tree needs to be managed manually. This means that if you developed a script to create/manage resources, you as an engineer need to order the commands sequentially. To solve such problems and neatly manage everything, you need a solution that can make the creation of resources organized, template-based, customizable, and controlled via a state. IaC solves these problems.

In today's world, everyone wants to adopt or migrate to the cloud. More and more organizations are following the cloud-native approach where they are either cloud-based from day one or are transforming their workloads to run on the cloud. Even for those companies who are reluctant to move to a public cloud, there is still a shift to a private cloud. In a nutshell, cloud computing transforms engineering and technology to a new level and impacts industries.

Whether a public or private cloud, whenever a user needs something, they use an offering or service in the cloud. For example, if a user needs a Linux server, they need a virtual machine on the cloud, which falls under the IaaS (infrastructure as a service) model. A cloud provider's primary role is to provide a wide variety of services to the user to meet their needs and requirements. Now say a user has chosen to use X number of cloud services, and for simplicity, let's assume the cloud provider is GCP (Google Cloud Platform). To get those services, the user has to do the following.

1. Choose the appropriate services from a catalog.

2. Create an instance of every service the user needs for their use case.

3. Configure the instances of the service.

4. Prepare to fine-tune/modify the configuration on an as-needed basis.

Now imagine that the needs of the user increase, and they need the following.

- All the services are created again for different environments (e.g., development, preproduction, etc.).

- The solution supports multiple clouds and creates similar services (e.g., AWS, Azure, etc.).

- Increase the resources allocated for service Y in environment A and make it minimal for the dev environment.

As you see in this example, there is the same issue regarding management and scalability. There is an offering to solve such problems, which falls under the IaC model.

IaC Solutions

The IaC model means that instead of doing everything manually, you create a set of code/scripts, which can also be referred to as templates. These scripts can make all the services a user needs on the cloud for running the desired workload/applications. IaC solutions are developed by every cloud provider, such as GCP cloud deployment manager, Azure ARM templates, OpenStack Heat, and AWS CodeDeploy.

Terraform is an IaC offering that provides the following advantages.

- **Agnostic**: It is cloud agnostic and can support almost all popular cloud providers.

- **State**: It can store the state of the created infrastructure on the cloud on which the workloads are running.

- **Resource tree mapping**: It maintains a graph schema internally that tells which resources are dependent, making the user free from the task of mapping resources.

- **Extendable**: The functionality of TF (Terraform) can be extended, which means the user can create their modules and providers.

- **Incremental upgrades**: TF analyzes all the changes users make to the scripts and only applies those changes.

- **Platform independent**: TF is a small CLI utility installed on Windows, OS X, or Linux, or even run as a Docker container.

- **Secure**: It connects to configured cloud providers securely via API keys or token-based authentication. In GCP, service accounts are also supported.

Terraform is not developed by any cloud provider. Terraform aims to support all clouds. It is quite popular and is used widely as a preferred IaC solution. You already have a K8s cluster you are experimenting with. Do the following to get familiar with Terraform.

1. Delete your K8s cluster.

2. Delete all the resources that you created for the K8s cluster.

3. Use Terraform to create all resources.

4. Observe the change of process in creation of cluster when done via Terraform.

I use GCP as the cloud provider, so the commands might differ from yours; it depends on your chosen cloud provider. Running the following commands deletes the resources you created for the exercise.

- **gcloud container clusters delete my-cluster**

- **gcloud compute networks delete my-network**

Now the next part is to make all these resources via Terraform. It is a templating library, so you never specify the values while writing code for creating resources. All the values come from dynamic variables and can be selected at runtime or via a variable file. There are four major steps in creating resources via Terraform.

1. **Authenticate.** Terraform needs to connect to the cloud provider to create resources. In GCP, the recommended way is to create a service account (SA) and then provide it to Terraform. It is recommended because you can assign specific roles. This prevents giving access to resources that are not to be used. Service accounts have key-based authentication, and JSON files store the keys, which then communicate to the GCP cloud. A basic declaration of service accounts looks like the following.

   ```
   resource "google_service_account" "default" {
           account_id = "service-account-id"
           display_name = "Service Account"
       }
   ```

2. **Resource definition.** Whatever resource you want to create, you have to provide the resource type and in the block, define the different attributes such as the name, location, and flavor. Every resource has

different attributes and is generally described in the documentation. In GCP, the managed K8s solution is GKE, so you create a GKE resource. The following is a sample snippet of GKE.

```
resource "google_container_cluster"
"primary" {
    name = "my-gke-cluster"
    location = "us-central1"
    initial_node_count = 1 }
```

In this example, the attribute values are defined. But, in actual scenarios, you use variables instead of values to make it look like a generic template that can create as many GKEs as you want. You can even extend it by building the module, which is more advanced. This is covered in later sections.

3. **Plan your infrastructure.** Whatever resources you create on any cloud, always remember that it involves cost. It is always good to make sure that you validate your templates and cross-check what resources you are creating on the cloud. This is known as the *planning phase*, where Terraform shows you the changes done to the infrastructure. Terraform maintains a state of whatever it does, so if you alter some things in resources and rerun the plan, it automatically finds the incremental changes and does only. The command is **terraform plan -o myplan**, where **myplan** is the plan file name.

4. **Apply changes.** This is the final part where the
    plan created in step 3 makes the changes on the
    configured cloud provider. Once the changes are
    applied, the job is finished, and the resources
    have been successfully created. The command
    to do this is **terraform apply "myplan"**, where
    myplan is the name of the plan file built during the
    planning phase.

Now you know the basics of Terraform and how it works.

Let's create a K8s cluster you need for later exercises. Next is a working
example of Terraform scripts that I have used to get a GKE cluster on GCP.

Working with Terraform

Let's use sample scripts to create a GKE cluster using Terraform. Before
moving to the template parts, let's first look at how to deploy a simple GKE
cluster. You need to know about the following.

- A **VPC network** is the network in which GKE is created

- A **node pool** contains the nodes that make up the data
  plane of the cluster.

- A **service account** attaches to the cluster's nodes.

- **Node config** means the resources that every node has
  in terms of CPU, memory, RAM, HDD, and so on.

- The **location** is the zone where the cluster is deployed.
  (Since this is for testing purposes, you are deploying a
  zonal cluster and not a regional cluster. In production,
  a multiregional cluster is recommended.)

With all that in mind, let's now look at the following template.

```
===============================================================
resource "google_service_account" "default" {
  account_id   = "service-account-id"
  display_name = "Service Account"
}

resource "google_compute_network" "vpc_network" {
  name = "vpc-network"
}

resource "google_container_cluster" "primary" {
  name                = "mycluster"
  location            = "us-central1-a"
  initial_node_count = 3
  Network = vpc_network.id
  node_config {
    service_account = google_service_account.default.email
    oauth_scopes = [
      "https://www.googleapis.com/auth/cloud-platform"
    ]
    labels = {
      foo = "bar"
    }
    tags = ["foo", "bar"]
  }
  timeouts {
    create = "30m"
    update = "40m"
  }
}
===============================================================
```

If you closely observe this snippet, you notice that whatever was done via CLI is the same, but this time instead of running the command, the infrastructure is defined in a file. Under the hood, Terraform is calling the same APIs that the gcloud CLI is calling. It's just that the interface is now enabling the user to do everything in a much more programmatic and organized way.

The power is not in the script but in how much you can customize it. For example, let's look at another snippet where the values have been replaced with vars in Terraform.

```
=============================================================
resource "google_service_account" "default" {
  account_id   = "service-account-id"
  display_name = "Service Account"
}

resource "google_compute_network" "vpc_network" {
  name = var.network_name
}

resource "google_container_cluster" "primary" {
  name                = var.cluster_name
  location            =  var.location
  initial_node_count = var.node_count
  Network             = vpc_network.id
  node_config {
    service_account = google_service_account.default.email
    oauth_scopes = [
      "https://www.googleapis.com/auth/cloud-platform"
    ]
    labels = var.labels
    tags = var.tags
  }
```

```
  timeouts {
    create = "30m"
    update = "40m"
  }
}
```

===

The only difference in this template is that there are no values provided here; instead, the variables are assigned to the value fields. There is another file known as **terraform.tfvars**, which looks like the following.

===

```
network_name = "test"
cluster_name = "mycluster"
location = "us-west1-c"
node_count  = 3
labels = {
  foo: "bar"
}
tags = ["foo", "bar"]
```

===

This enables you to create a generic code that creates a GKE cluster and then supplies the variable files as per the environment. It makes the code scalable, and it is a cleaner way to manage the infrastructure.

State Management

Once Terraform creates infrastructure, it creates a state file locally that the tool uses to determine the infrastructure present on the cloud and what to create/delete. The state file is very important and is used by Terraform CLI while starting. Consider a team of engineers who maintain and manage the infrastructure since the state file is created locally.

To solve this issue, Terraform supports keeping state files in cloud providers' object storage, such as GCS and S3 buckets. Whenever Terraform runs, it fetches the state file from a backend which can be a bucket present in cloud storage. There should be a bucket.tf file in your project to enable this feature. A typical **backend.tf** looks something like the following.

```
terraform {
  backend "gcs" {
    bucket  = "tf-state-prod"
    prefix  = "terraform/state"
  }
}
```

Here the back end is Google Cloud Storage (GCS), and the bucket name is **tf-state-prod.** Whenever CLI runs, it fetches the state file from this bucket.

Service Mesh

Modern systems are often built as distributed collections of microservices, with each microservice providing a specific business function. A service mesh is a specialized infrastructure layer that you can incorporate into your apps. It lets you add features like observability, traffic management, and security to your code without changing it.

The term *service mesh* refers to the software that you use to implement this design and the security or network domain generated when you do so.

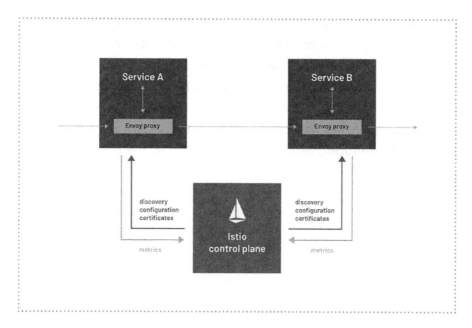

Figure 4-2. *Control plane of Istio*

It can become more difficult to comprehend and manage distributed service deployments as they expand in size and complexity, such as a Kubernetes-based system. Discovery, load balancing, failure recovery, metrics, and monitoring are some of the needs. A service mesh often addresses more complex operational requirements, like A/B testing, canary deployments, rate limiting, access control, encryption, and end-to-end authentication.

Summary

This chapter broadly discussed how to write code for creating infrastructure instead of using CLI. You also learned why IaC is important and the problems it tries to address. Along with that, you played with Terraform and had a step-by-step explanation of what Terraform does.

On the other hand, Helm charts come to the rescue only when deploying applications on Kubernetes. A service mesh is a special solution that solves networking problems between microservices. It helps you understand, segregate, scale and secure the inflow and outflow of traffic between microservices.

Let's proceed to one of the most important aspects of any application: security and monitoring.

CHAPTER 5

Security and Monitoring

To summarize the key takeaways, you now have practical knowledge of working on a Kubernetes cluster, developing and deploying applications from scratch, and integrating CI/CD practices in the software development life cycle (SDLC). Along with it, you also know how to make an infrastructure scalable and organized using IaC templates. To add a cherry on top, all this knowledge is language agnostic and can be applied no matter what kind of language, nature, or domain your software belongs to. But an application's and a system's journey are never considered complete without security and monitoring. Once the software reaches a release phase and goes for audit by the security and operations team, the engineering team is flooded by the following questions.

- How do you secure public-facing applications?

- How can the security of a system be compromised?

- How do you make sure the application data is never leaked?

- How do you check that the application's services are healthy?

- How is authentication happening?

© Prateek Khushalani 2022
P. Khushalani, *Kubernetes Application Developer*,
https://doi.org/10.1007/978-1-4842-8032-4_5

The list of questions can be endless, but as an engineer, you have to make sure the environment you are deploying your applications on is secured in the best possible manner. Remember that security is one of the top priorities and should not be left behind. When applications are deployed on a public cloud, it becomes extremely important that all the policies and best practices are used for securing the application/services. Before jumping to how to secure and monitor applications running on a Kubernetes cluster, let's discuss the concepts first. Understanding the concepts is very important. That tells you that, although it's all the same at the base, cloud systems have made security and monitoring a shared responsibility.

Figure 5-1. *Security in the cloud*

Traditional Applications

Security and monitoring concepts generally remain the same in the computing domain, but how and where to apply them varies by the system an application is running on. To explain this with an example, consider that you, as a developer, built a monolithic application. The nature of this application is public facing, and users access the application via a web URL `https://mymonilithicapp.com`. The application provides a chat system where all the users who are logged in can communicate with each other by exchanging messages. Figure 5-2 illustrates a basic view of this application.

Traditional Chat Application

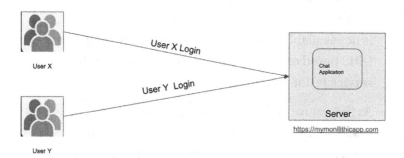

Figure 5-2. *Basic chat application (monolithic)*

I won't go into concepts like networking, data center location, or routing because the goal is to focus on security and monitoring. Being monolithic and traditional, the following are part of application development.

- **Authentication and authorization**: Not everyone should be able to access the chat console. First, check if the users exist in the DB or not

- **Access control**: Allows only a subset of users to access the application. For example, there can be users like admin, general, group-user, auditor, and so forth.

111

- **Certificate management**: The interface is a URL, and the clients access the application via a browser. In this case, no one likes to visit a non-encrypted HTTP-based address. So, the application needs to bind to SSL certificates and check if the certs are valid and are signed by a trusted certificate authority (CA).

- **Cyberattacks**: A public address on the Internet can be accessed by anyone across the globe. Even if you open your application to a particular region, the URL is still accessible across the globe. From an application perspective, a check can find the clients' region and display a banner stating, "Service is not available." This is a very common practice where say, if Netflix is not available in your region, you can still open the URL. Based on your region, Netflix reports that the service is not available.

  As the nature of the chat application is public, it is under a constant threat of attacks like distributed denial-of-service (DDoS), cross-site scripting, and SQL injection. There is a standard document for developers known as OWASP Top 10. It lists the ten most critical security risks to web applications. All of this has to be taken care of in the application itself. From a data center perspective, some security features might be provided at the load balancer level, but the software must still handle it.

- **Health**: This becomes a concern when there is significant traffic and flow of messages between users. The software has to report high resource usage in terms of CPU, memory, HDD, and network to the systems provided by the operations team. The operations team can put more servers so that the load can be better distributed and handled.

As you can see, there are a lot of factors for which a significant amount of development is required in the chat application as it's working in a standalone fashion. Why discuss such a scenario if no one builds monolithic software? How is it related in the context of the cloud? The chat application was conceptually doing the following things at the conceptual level.

- Access management

- Role-based access control mechanism

- Enabling TLS by configuring certificates

- Handling of threats

- Monitoring and reporting application status

You might be astonished to hear that even though that chat application was monolithic, the key things it was trying to achieve for security and monitoring conceptually remain the same even when your applications run on the cloud. To illustrate this, let's build the same chat application but this time in a modernized way where everything is cloud native.

Cloud-Based Applications

Let's build a chat-based web application on the cloud. The nature and audience of the application remain the same, so you can directly dive into how it looks from an architectural standpoint. Figure 5-3 illustrates a view of the application running on the cloud.

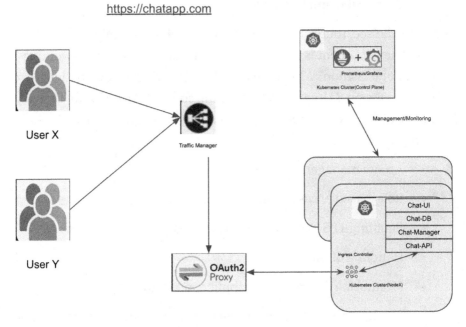

Figure 5-3. *Cloud-based chat application*

The first difference you notice is that there are many components compared to the traditional one. Here the chat application is a part of the system, and the application itself is broken into several microservices where every service has its own job. For example, Chat-UI is a dynamic website that gets data from Chat-API. But since the focus is more on security and monitoring, let's discover what has changed.

- **Threat handling**: If you notice the traffic is first landing on a component known as the *traffic manager*. It acts as an entrypoint and is responsible for routing the traffic to the correct endpoint. Also, this component must follow all the Top 10 OWASP security standards. One very good example is the GCP's L7 HTTP load balancer with Google Cloud Armor; the load balancer routes traffic, and Cloud Armor prevents cyberattacks.

- **Authorization and access**: Traffic lands to OAuth2 Proxy after the traffic manager. OAuth2 is an industry standard authorization protocol. OAuth2 Proxy is an open source software that can be hooked like a plug-and-play component. Its role is to authorize the users via a list of supported providers and provide a JWT (JSON Web Token) with user details like first name, last name, and picture, along with the groups the user is part of.

- **Monitoring and alerting**: Kubernetes clusters support integration with various monitoring and alerting systems. One such system is Prometheus and Grafana. Their job is simple, to monitor the resource usage of the Pods running on the cluster and show visualizations of usage in a GUI. Prometheus specifically works on the part of collecting the metrics, and Grafana works on GUI visualizations and dashboards. Using these built-in tools of the system, rules can be created based on which the Pods can be scaled vertically or horizontally to meet sudden load spikes. Figure 5-4 shows a sample Grafana dashboard displaying the status of Kubernetes Pods.

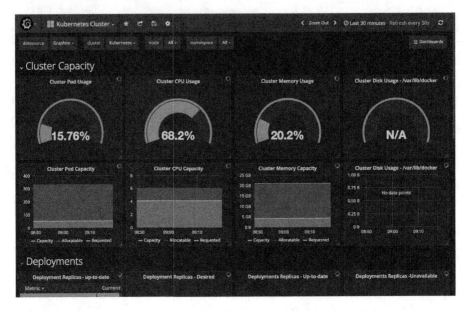

Figure 5-4. *Grafana sample dashboard*

I have neglected the chat application while discussing all these points since all those aspects are handled outside the application. This truly tells what it means when you say that security in the cloud is a joint responsibility.

Security in Kubernetes

Kubernetes and a wide variety of plugins make the life of an engineer simple. But configuring K8s can sometimes become challenging and tedious since there are many best practices you have to follow. To make things a bit more complex, every cloud provider offers a managed K8s solution, and each provider has its own set of best practices that the deployment engineer should follow. But at the core level, it's the same K8s cluster, so there are some best practices to make sure no matter which solution you choose or even if you deploy and manage it yourself in an on-prem environment, your cluster is secured. The applications running on it are safe from attacks.

Kubernetes is a complex platform and requires extensive configuration and management. To keep Kubernetes workloads safe, especially in a production environment, you must address key architectural vulnerabilities and platform dependencies by implementing security best practices. To make things simple, you can divide the security into two parts: the cluster level and the application level. If you are interested in doing it as you read, make sure you have access to your Kubernetes cluster and kubectl commands are working. Also, make sure that you have full access to the cluster, as there might be some admin commands running as you progress. With that in mind, let's start with the cluster level.

Cluster-Level Practices

Version Upgrades

K8s is software composed of an API, scheduler, controller, and many plugins, so it becomes important to update the Kubernetes cluster itself. The control plane is the most important part here as you connect and manage the cluster via the control plane.

Every quarterly update adds new security features, not just bug fixes. To take advantage of them, you should run the latest stable version. The best thing to do is run the latest release with its most recent patches. If you are managing a K8s cluster yourself, then this part is for you, the managed K8s services provided by cloud providers automatically handle this. Still, as an engineer, you should be aware of it even if not doing it yourself.

Figure 5-5. *Secure K8S*

A word of caution: if you are managing your own K8s cluster and are patching/upgrading the cluster regularly, then please make sure you have a control plane in high availability mode, as during an upgrade, the control plane goes into maintenance mode and might even break and stop working. Also, there is an upgrade ladder which means you cannot upgrade from any version. It is maintained by the community and published at `https://kubernetes.io/releases/version-skew-policy/`.

Also, one thing to note is that you should always back up all the resources, such as the manifest files, which are generally present under **/etc/kubernetes/manifests** directory. Along with the manifest files, remember that the database for K8s is ***etcd,*** so it becomes extremely important to back up the schema and data of the database. I recommend having a sound experience with **etcd** so that you can connect to etcd and see the data stored in the **K8s** cluster yourself. Again, this is necessary only for users who manage the K8s cluster themselves and are not using any managed service solution.

Use of Namespaces

As K8s is a collection of nodes that can range from a few to thousands, a single cluster can be home to thousands of services running on these nodes. Every service running on the cluster is unique and has its own requirements. Generally, when an application is deployed on K8s, it is composed of many services. In the last chapter, you created a SaaS book store comprising four or five services where each service was running on a K8s cluster. All these services had some configuration and networking policies. From a scaling perspective, it has some rules to handle traffic spikes and a quota by which you specify how much you should scale at max.

There is a lot of configuration for a single application. Imagine a K8s cluster hosting thousands of applications. It would be cluttered and a nightmare for the monitoring and ops team to manage the cluster. Enter namespaces to the rescue. Namespace offers an isolated area where you can host all your configuration, services, secrets, and eventually, all the K8s objects. This doesn't mean that each namespace gets a dedicated node, but it makes things organized and simpler to manage many applications running on K8s. It is much easier to apply security controls such as network policies when different types of workloads are deployed in separate namespaces.

Special Workloads

Sometimes, some applications/workloads have special demands due to security reasons or different requirements, such as GPU or hardware architecture. It can also be OS specific where your application can run only on a particular operating system. You need a dedicated hardware/node to run your workloads/applications in such cases.

Along with namespaces, you can use taints, tolerations, and node affinity to make sure such workloads always run on the dedicated host. You can also configure K8s affinity rules so that no normal workload can be scheduled on such dedicated nodes.

Container Registries

Everything that runs on K8s is in the form of a container. What it means is that all applications are packaged in a container. Then images of these packaged applications are stored in a container registry which is pulled when the application runs on the K8s cluster. The contents of this image depend on what kind of application it is for. A React application, for example, has the Node.js libraries and the modules that the app needs to run.

Similarly, if you have a Golang/C/C++ application, it has a binary, and the image can be a busybox because everything is bundled in the application's binary. Organizations need strong governance policies regarding how images are built and stored in trusted image registries. You must ensure that container images are built using secure and approved base images that are regularly scanned. Only images from image registries on allow lists are used to launch containers in your Kubernetes environment.

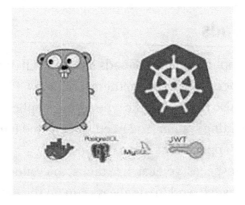

Figure 5-6. *Container Images*

Vulnerability scanning is of utmost importance as if there is malicious software in the image which eventually is used to run a workload on K8s. It can impact not only the application but the cluster as well.

RBAC

Role-based access control is a mechanism by which you restrict the user's access by the role assigned to it or to the group to which the user belongs. Giving access to all the namespaces to an application developer makes no sense. The developer can see the applications he is working on and the system services and other applications running on the cluster. It is always advised to provide namespace level access to the user where they can manage only what can run inside their assigned namespace. Any system command is not allowed, and the user gets a **403 Forbidden** error.

RBAC is usually enabled by default in Kubernetes 1.6 and beyond (later for some managed providers). But, if you have upgraded since then and haven't changed your configuration, you'll want to double-check your settings. Because of the way Kubernetes authorization controllers are combined, you must both enable RBAC and disable legacy attribute-based access control (ABAC).

Once RBAC is being enforced, you still need to use it effectively. Cluster-wide permissions should generally be avoided in favor of namespace-specific permissions. Avoid giving anyone cluster admin privileges, even for debugging — it is much more secure to grant access only as needed on a case-by-case basis. You can explore the cluster roles and roles using `**kubectl get clusterrolebinding**` or `**kubectl get rolebinding –all-namespaces**`.

Network Policies

As K8s is a single cluster and can be home to thousands of applications, it becomes a problem if an application becomes notorious and communicates with other applications residing in another namespace. Also, if a workload gets hacked or due to some issues, it pulls large chunks of data from the public Internet, which can choke your entire network bandwidth.

Based on these cases, two major things were touched on here with respect to networking: authorized/restricted access, where a service can only communicate to those services which it should, and when it comes to access to the Internet, allow that or maybe set QoS policies to limit the bandwidth allocated to every service.

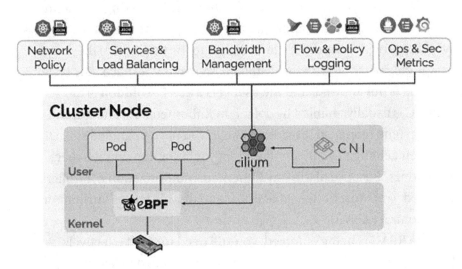

Figure 5-7. *Flow Control*

Even if you have not installed plugins like Istio for advanced networking configuration and management, K8s provides a rich set of network policies that can be applied. Although Kubernetes always supports operations on the ***NetworkPolicy*** resource, simply creating the resource without a plugin that implements it has no effect. Example plugins include Calico, Cilium, Kube-router, Romana, and Weave Net.

Network policies get applied at the Pod level, and to apply a network policy, you need to specify the podSelector field. Each network policy specifies a list of allowed (ingress and egress) connections. When the network policy is created, all the Pods that it applies to are allowed to make or accept the connections listed in it. In other words, a network policy is essentially a list of allowed connections; a connection to or from a Pod is allowed if it is permitted by at least one of the network policies that apply to the Pod.

The best approach is to follow the least possible allowance where you close every possible door and allow only those connections which are legit. If you are doing this on the running cluster, then there is a good chance that all the applications in the cluster will stop running. Don't panic because initially, this might sound like a bad plan, but when you know which service needs what connectivity and why, it gives you an in-depth understanding of your cluster and its applications.

You start by removing **ingress** or inbound traffic from the Internet completely for all the Pods. Apply a ***default-deny-all*** network policy. The effect of the following policy specification is to isolate *all* Pods, which means that only connections explicitly listed by other network policies are allowed.

```
apiVersion: networking.k8s.io/v1
kind: NetworkPolicy
metadata:
 name: default-deny-all
spec:
 podSelector: {}
 policyTypes:
 - Ingress
```

One of the other advantages of this policy is that it is not applied to a specific Pod or object on K8s. You can consider this a wild card policy, which means that even if a Pod gets deleted or created, this policy is not affected and is applied to all by default.

Note   Since network policies are namespaced resources, you need to create this policy for each namespace. You can do so by running kubectl -n <namespace> create -f <filename> for each namespace.

Allow Internet Access

Once this policy is applied, no Pod can get traffic from the Internet. How do you make some of the Pods access the Internet? The answer is simple: create another network policy for the specific Pod. Also, note that this removes the connectivity between Pods, so even those services that need to talk to each other break.

One thing which is the thumb rule in K8s is the system of labels. The key to understanding which object is mapped or associated with which other object is via labels. In network policy, you create a policy to enable Internet access to Pods not by explicitly providing each Pod's name but by creating a label and then making sure all the Pods that need access have that label. The following is a network policy to allow Internet access.

```
apiVersion: networking.k8s.io/v1
kind: NetworkPolicy
metadata:
 name: internet-access
spec:
 podSelector:
   matchLabels:
     networking/allow-internet-access: "true"
 policyTypes:
 - Ingress
 ingress:
 - {}
```

One thing to note is the label created: **allow-internet access**. This means that all the Pods with this label have this network policy attached. It is a powerful feature of K8s, making the entire system scale massively. You group items not by individually adding them but by labeling them with easy and memorable names.

Inter-Pod Communication

Now let's move to another scenario where you want to allow Pods to talk to each other. There are two ways of doing this. The basic one is where you don't know which Pods are talking to each other. In this case, you can create another wild card policy where you enable inter-Pod communication for an entire namespace. The following is an example.

```
apiVersion: networking.k8s.io/v1
kind: NetworkPolicy
metadata:
 name: allow-same-namespace
spec:
 podSelector: {}
 policyTypes:
 - Ingress
 ingress:
 - from:
   - podSelector: {}
```

podSelector is set to {}, which means that all Pods are accepted. There is nothing specific to filter with respect to which Pods need access to other Pods in the namespace. This is simple but does not have any granularity because if there are x Pods in a namespace, then all those Pods can talk to each other.

Now let's move to a case where you know which Pod needs to talk to whom. Assume an Apache Kafka server is running. It is used by many other services running as separate Pods; so it is a many-to-one or a hub-and-spoke system where Kafka is the hub, and all the services need to connect to it. Make sure you have a label such as **app=kafka** attached to your Kafka Pod, and then you can enable access to Kafka from your Pods by having a label such as **networking/allow-kafka-access=true**. Your policy should look something like the following.

```
apiVersion: networking.k8s.io/v1
kind: NetworkPolicy
metadata:
 name: allow-db-access
spec:
 podSelector:
   matchLabels:
     app: "db"
 policyTypes:
 - Ingress
 ingress:
 - from:
   - podSelector:
       matchLabels:
         networking/allow-db-access: "true"
```

The following are the key points about network policies.

- Block everything by default.

- Identify which Pod needs connectivity to what and why.

- Create labels and attach them to Pods.

- Use those labels to create network policies.

- Use global policies that are not attached to a Pod so that they don't get removed when the Pod is deleted.

Runtime Users and Groups

A container runs an application in an isolated namespace and shares the underlying kernel of the host operating system. The application running inside the container is a process that runs with a user and group ID. If you create a container image and run an application, you will likely run it as a root user, which is the default behavior.

This part is often missed, and if the application runs as a root user, then the application can do almost anything sometimes, even at the cluster level. One such bug was the dirty copy-on-write, which is not directly related to the root user but explains that if the container user is the root, writing on the mounted volume is allowed even though it is mounted in read-only mode. More information is at `https://blog.aquasec.com/dirty-cow-vulnerability-impact-on-containers`.

Even though it is important from a scalability perspective, you can't regularly check if a running Pod has a container that is running as a non-root user or not. There is a feature in K8s known as admission controllers to solve this problem. Using admission controllers, you can create specific requirements that every Pod should meet before being admitted to the cluster. You can set things like allowing a Pod to run only when UID/GID is between 10 and 1000, so any Pod trying to run as a root user does not start because it fails to meet the admission requirements of the cluster.

Monitoring in Kubernetes

Creating and deploying an application is simply one aspect of the CI/CD process in DevOps. Application monitoring is essential for ensuring that your application is constantly online and functioning properly. Effective application monitoring gathers comprehensive data about the program and metrics linked to operating systems, such as CPU and memory usage and storage consumption, to continually examine the condition of the application and the underlying infrastructure.

Prometheus is an open source application monitoring system that uses a simple text-based metrics format to help you manage huge amounts of data quickly. You can present data and handle alerts using a powerful query language. Prometheus integrates with Grafana for a graphical dashboard and PageDuty and Slack for alert alerts, among other things. Databases, server applications, Kubernetes, and Java virtual machines are among the products supported by Prometheus.

This section demonstrated how to use Docker and Helm in a cloud environment to solve application monitoring for a Spring Boot application. Prometheus does not come installed in a vanilla Kubernetes cluster. First, let's set up Prometheus.

Setting up Prometheus

1. Create a new namespace named monitoring by using the following command.

    `kubectl create namespace monitoring`

2. Create a file named clusterRole.yaml, and copy the following RBAC role.

    ```
    apiVersion: rbac.authorization.k8s.io/v1
    kind: ClusterRole
    metadata:
    ```

```yaml
  name: prometheus
rules:
- apiGroups: [""]
  resources:
  - nodes
  - nodes/proxy
  - services
  - endpoints
  - pods
  verbs: ["get", "list", "watch"]
- apiGroups:
  - extensions
  resources:
  - ingresses
  verbs: ["get", "list", "watch"]
- nonResourceURLs: ["/metrics"]
  verbs: ["get"]
---
apiVersion: rbac.authorization.k8s.io/v1
kind: ClusterRoleBinding
metadata:
  name: prometheus
roleRef:
  apiGroup: rbac.authorization.k8s.io
  kind: ClusterRole
  name: prometheus
subjects:
- kind: ServiceAccount
  name: default
  namespace: monitoring
```

3. Create the role by using the following command.

   kubectl create -f clusterRole.yaml

4. Create a config map via the following command.

   kubectl create -f https://raw.
   githubusercontent.com/bibinwilson/
   kubernetes-prometheus/master/config-map.yaml

5. The config map contains all the configurations to dynamically discover Pods and services running in the Kubernetes cluster.

6. Create a Prometheus deployment via the following command.

   kubectl create -f https://raw.
   githubusercontent.com/prateek2408/
   BookExamples/main/prometheus-deployment.yaml

7. Check the deployment by using the following command.

   kubectl get deployments --namespace=monitoring

   If you have Kubernetes Dashboard enabled, you can also select the monitoring namespace, which presents something like what's shown in Figure 5-8.

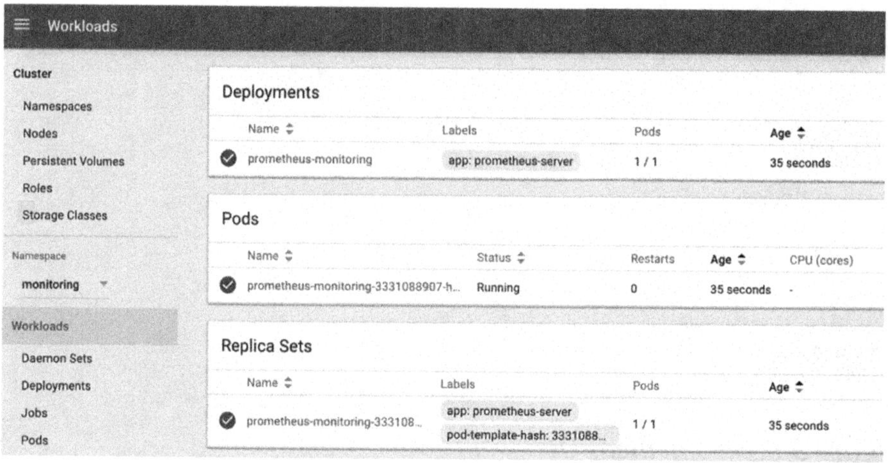

Figure 5-8. *Prometheus deployment*

8. To access the Prometheus UI, you need to expose the deployment via a service. Run the following command to do that.

kubectl create -f https://raw. githubusercontent.com/prateek2408/ BookExamples/main/prometheus-service.yaml

9. Assuming Kubernetes is running locally, go to http://localhost:30000 in your browser to open the Prometheus UI, as shown in Figure 5-9.

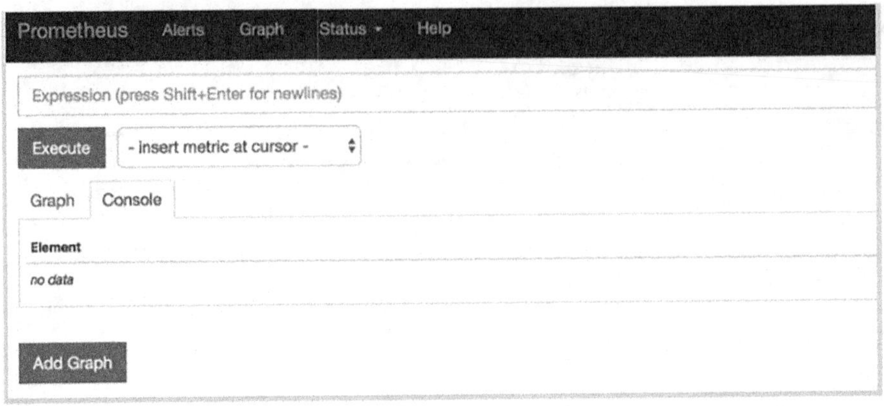

Figure 5-9. *Prometheus UI*

Configuring an Application

Generally, no modification is needed for sending data to Prometheus. Since the monitoring system automatically discovers the Pods running in the namespace, metrics like how many requests are going to the application are automatically fetched. Resource usage like CPU, memory, HDD, and network is also noted at a Pod level, so modification is needed at the application level. However, some frameworks like Spring Boot in Java provide a way to add support for Prometheus.

If you check the Prometheus docs, you find that Prometheus recommends adding JMX Exporter to Java-based applications. This example adds JMX Exporter by doing the following.

1. Create a file and name it **logging.properties** with
    the following content.

```
=============================================
handlers=java.util.logging.ConsoleHandler
java.util.logging.ConsoleHandler.level=ALL
io.prometheus.jmx.level=ALL
io.prometheus.jmx.shaded.io.prometheus.jmx.level=ALL
=============================================
```

2. When starting the application, provide the file in the
    flags like the following.

```
=============================================
-Djava.util.logging.config.file=/path/to/logging.properties
=============================================
```

This makes the Java application aware of Prometheus, and the
application framework starts exporting the logs to Prometheus. Remember
that the integration to Prometheus is language and framework specific,
though, without the integration, you still get the basic metrics about the
application. But if you want to get very fine level metrics, check out support
for your language and framework. For example, if you want to integrate
Prometheus to a front-end app developed in React, **@cabify/prom-react**
enables you to get metrics like the rate per second per page.

Summary

Security and monitoring are two pillars that help secure and run your application in a scalable fashion. In today's world, the application development and future are not decided only by the engineering team but are also data-driven. Decisions like clicks per second, bounce rate, how many unique users are coming, errors faced, and regions from where traffic is coming help make future judgments. No matter how advanced or problem-solving your application is, no one would trust it if it's not secure enough. For example, consider an application that stores users' personal information and food habits and generates a diet chart that the users find extremely helpful. The users for this application are growing, which is very good, but suddenly there is a data breach, and all the users' data is now leaked.

This breach would be a tremendous loss to the application as even though the application security gets fixed, no one would trust the application. Furthermore, security attacks that compromise the application leave a tough spot to remove. Therefore, it is always good to keep the application's security of utmost importance. If you start considering security aspects at the time of development, it makes the application sealed and less prone to attacks.

With that in mind, let's head to the next chapter, where you build a SaaS-based solution from scratch. You use all the knowledge you have gained in the next chapter to create this application. It is a cloud-native application where the users can see the review of books.

CHAPTER 6

Building a SaaS Solution

The previous chapters have gone through the building block modules on security, monitoring, deployment, storage, networking, and computing. This chapter brings every module together to build a SaaS solution from scratch. Everything that you have learned from this book is tested here as you solve an actual use case in which you design, develop, test, deploy and release software as a SaaS-based solution. While doing this, leverage what you can from the cloud offerings and build only the pieces which add value to the product. The cloud is all about not reinventing the wheel and focusing on the core idea or business logic to make your product a proper cloud-native solution that is easy to deploy, integrate, scale, and cost-effective.

© Prateek Khushalani 2022
P. Khushalani, *Kubernetes Application Developer*,
https://doi.org/10.1007/978-1-4842-8032-4_6

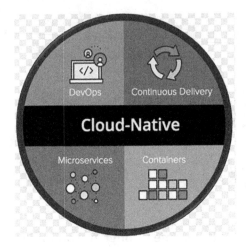

Figure 6-1. *Cloud-native practices Source:*

Overview

Let's first discuss what a SaaS solution is. SaaS stands for *software as a service* and is one of the offerings on the cloud. Office 365 is an example of a SaaS-based solution provided by Microsoft where a user can use any of its services from anywhere across the globe by just using a thin client. In the SaaS-based model, the entire software and its services are running on the cloud. The user needs a client to access the software and start consuming it. Billing is generally on a usage/subscription basis, and the software itself is multi-tenant so that multiple organizations can use the same solution. The organization providing the solution takes care of things like privacy, data protection, authorization, and backup. Essential features like an upgrade, uptime, and maintenance also fall under the organization owning the solution. The users have almost nothing to do apart from consuming the software services.

Figure 6-2. *SaaS solutions*

As the SaaS solution takes almost all the huddles away from the end user, designing a SaaS solution is complex and challenging. It has to cover almost everything ranging from computation to security. Careful steps and time is taken in designing a SaaS solution. The engineers have to brainstorm and find all possible cases in the solution as if there are any blocks left to be covered. It can cause a significant blocker/loss in the long run. Imagine a SaaS solution that is very secure and compliant with almost all the standards but is too slow. That won't work.

Figure 6-3. *Types of SaaS solutions*

Phase Development

Remember, it is impossible to design a full-proof solution when you run it. There are new cases that were never discovered during the designing phase. There is always a *proof of concept* (POC) done initially to narrow down these cases, which can then be rectified by altering the design used to create a POC. Generally, only a couple of engineers try to bring up the solution in the least possible effort and mimic if the solution is feasible. The POC is a significant phase as this brings your design to life in a concise timeline. It helps you redesign your solution to make it robust. If the design is not feasible and POC fails, then a decision can be taken to scrap the use case or design it again. The thumb rule is to have a POC with the initial design to validate it and generally not take the entire team on it as this is just a concept phase and nothing is certain at this point.

Figure 6-4. *POC phase of an application*

Once the POC passes and the design is intact, you are all good to make it a product. The team for its development is then involved. Using the Agile business model, create EPICS, user stories, tasks, and subtasks. The scrum master generally syncs with the Architect who has designed the software solution. Product development is the phase that starts the SDLC process where the engineers are educated about what they are building. The testing team is also involved at a high level to know what product they are testing. The product development phase is relatively less risky but time-consuming as creating the process, making everyone aware, and kickstarting the project take time.

Product Overview

You should now understand how things flow, so let's start and head to the part where you start building a SaaS solution. For this case, you are given a task where you have to develop a SaaS solution: a bookstore where any user can come to read a book by paying a monthly service. This SaaS solution allows any user to visit the web application's home page, sign up, pay for the service, and start using the portal to open any book in the store. Writers can upload their books to be available in the bookstore. An admin can delete books from the library. The following lists the essential items.

- SaaS solution to run an online bookstore

- Users can be of three types

  - A **reader** who reads the book

  - A **writer** who publishes books on the portal (there is an age restriction)

  - An **admin** who maintains the bookstore

- Users can sign up and pay monthly to read the books.

Let's begin the step-by-step design phase of the solution. The first thing to do is split each domain.

Authentication and Authorization

This is the entry phase, and users need to sign in or sign-up to get into the portal, so some authentication is needed. You also need to have roles for multiple types of users: reader, writer, and admin. As the solution grows, different types of readers, writers, and admins can have subcategories, such as super admin, book admin, or even book-content verifiers. These users can be roles in the system, where a user carries a role that identifies which type is entering the system. If new kinds of users pop up in the system, you can create new roles for them.

IAM, or *identity access management*, is the service that is available on almost all cloud providers and fits perfectly for this use case. There are also some other identity access providers like Auth0, which takes the part of access management and needs to be integrated via plugins into the system. IAM is a service given by the cloud, so every cloud provider such as

GCP, AWS, Azure, or IBM has a different approach. Choosing IAM from the cloud provider catalog helps delegate the Authorization, Authentication, and RBAC and focus more on the application's core business value.

Storage

The product deals with storing books and making the users read the book when they click it in the library. So the product majorly keeps the books, and object storage suits this use case as it is meant for multimedia files, and books are typically in pdfs and word format. In the storage module, you also have metadata containing data, such as the author, date of publication, and so forth. Metadata is required for indexing and searching the books. A sample pdf is stored to show a sneak peek of the book. All cloud providers provide block storage services, so you can directly consume this service for storing the data.

You need a database to handle application storage like a library, including the number of books and the titles displayed in the store. Let's use a simple MySQL database that every cloud provider provides in their cloud offering as a service. Using a managed service rather than creating a separate database instance is better as the cloud provider takes care of things like scaling, backup, and upgrade. When integrating with the application, you rely on the database SDK, as the solution should always be cloud-agnostic.

Computation

The business logic application, which consists of the UI, API, and some other services that are part of this solution, can all be in isolated containers so you can adapt the microservice architecture. One of the advantages of microservice architecture is that every service can be developed independently. Also, this gives a scope that if there is a fault with one component, it can be dealt with separately. If a new feature is needed, a new component can be added as a new microservice in the same system. Features like replication, load balancing, rollback, and blue-green deployment are needed. So you use a Kubernetes cluster for computation. Also, as every component is a separate service, they talk to each other via gRPC.

Infrastructure

To deploy the entire infra on a cloud, let's use Terraform because it is cloud-agnostic and gives you an IaC interface that can be stored like a code and then reused to create environments (e.g., dev, stage, prod, etc.). Finally, to deploy the application on the Kube cluster, you can create a helm chart and add it to a CI/CD pipeline.

Monitoring

Prometheus and Grafana become a robust monitoring system for a K8s cluster. Grafana dashboards are leveraged to display resource consumption, usage, and latency metrics. Dashboards and alerts can be set up if there is a problem with some service. Notifications can reach slack channels or even mails based upon preference.

Backup

Note the following product data.

- Application
  - Config files
  - Codebase
  - Metadata
  - Logs

- User data

  - Books

  - User information

The Pods on which the application run are stateless so that the configurations can come from the configMap Kube object. Backup of PV volumes is something that the cloud provider provides. Let's use GitHub for the codebase because they can ensure the codebase is backed up and available 24/7. For backup of logs again, you utilize cloud providers by leveraging their built-in services. Please note that the applications dump logs to either files or stdout, and the cloud provider has to scrape the records. You are not making changes in the codebase to support the cloud because the goal is to make the application as cloud-agnostic as possible.

Security

Every microservice starts TLS-enabled by default. The communication between microservices is always secured. Safety is the primary motto, right? To make a service spawn in a TLS-enabled fashion, you need certs. This means if you have ten services, ten certs are required because it's a 1-0-1 mapping. This way of running applications is not scalable as you have to manage these certs mapping, making it difficult and complex. You have previously learned about Istio and mTLS systems, so let's use them to make the communications TLS. Also, from the front-end perspective, the end user reaches the application via an address, and you use the ingress controllers in K8s, which listen only on 443 with no support for non-HTTPS traffic.

From the application and use case perspective, you are trying to visit every computing domain and solve how the system behaves and its features for a specific domain. For example, you now know that you use the RBAC system from the identity point of view, and the auth protocol is OAuth2. Similarly, all storage requirements use block storage services, and all the computation needs to happen on a container with Kubernetes as a *container orchestration engine* (COE). This exercise helps you identify the tools, technologies, and mechanisms involved in building this SaaS solution. Let's collect this information to create what's shown in Figure. 6-5

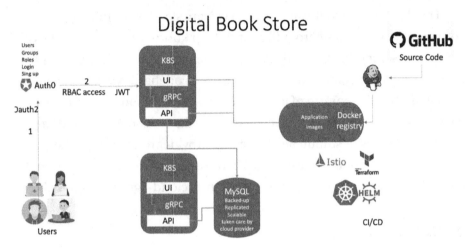

Figure 6-5. Digital bookstore

Everything I have discussed is shown in Figure 6-5. Creating a diagram is very important as it tells you if something is missing in the system. There are two K8s clusters in the diagram. Multiple clusters deal with situations where if one zone in a region fails, another site has the replica. So traffic can migrate from environment A to B. Setting up disaster recovery can be used for the blue-green technique. In a failure, if the application is not behaving correctly in environment A, traffic can be diverted to environment B. Everything is done via CI/CD pipelines. You can use tools like Travis and Jenkins to build pipelines and Terraform and Helm for deploying infrastructure. The source comes from GitHub, and based on branches and tags, the release is created.

In an actual scenario, many discussions and reviews happen, which is healthy because it helps tackle all the corner cases that get missed. Then the comments are incorporated into the product's design which creates new versions of the design documents. For example, the Docker registry was not mentioned during the initial discussions, so it was added to Figure 6-5 to mimic the scenario.

Let's do a fake review, where someone from the team points out that the registry is not being considered into the picture from a storage point of view. Take that review and add a Docker registry.

Now the design phase is complete so let's start with the implementation. There is a POC phase in an actual scenario, which is skipped in this book. POC is similar to the implementation phase, but less time is spent on quality; the plan is to bring the design to life as soon as possible. The goal of POC is to see if it's a feasible solution or not rather than ensuring all things are developed in order.

Suppose the POC phase is skipped in an actual scenario. In that case, there might be some major pitfalls in the implementation phase. For example, changing the design at the implementation phase is not a good idea as the entire team needs to be updated with the new design changes. Changing the design causes confusion and might also degrade the quality of development.

Implementing the Bookstore

Moving forward towards the implementation, let's do it step by step. And first, you need to create the infrastructure on the cloud provider you choose. For this chapter, I chose GCP, but you are free to choose any provider you want. For creating the resources on the cloud, you use Terraform and make everything in an IaC model. The scripts for creating the resources are present in the git repository under the tf directory and are working for GCP. If you use a different cloud, the scripts might not work as they need some changes. Link to the IaC code at `https://github.com/prateek2408/BookExamples/tree/main/tf`.

For the application to run, you need the following resources.

- **Kubernetes cluster**: A cluster on which the application runs in a microservice architecture. A managed service for K8s clusters in GCP is known as GKE (Google Kubernetes Engine). This managed service is used for this use case.

- **Container registry**: There needs to be a storehouse where all the container images are stored. Since all the microservices that run on the K8s cluster are containers, you need this service. GCR (Google Container Registry) is one such service where you can store all your container images. There is also Artifact Registry in GCP, which is the evolution of GCR.

- **Database**: You need a database to store all the user-related data and book information. GCP provides a managed service known as Cloud SQL for hosting MySQL DB.

Now that you know the resources you need, let's start creating them using Terraform. First, use **_terraform init, plan_** and **_apply_** to make the resources on the cloud. The code for creating resources is at `https://github.com/prateek2408/BookExamples/tree/main/tf`.

Once **terraform apply** is successful, you should see something similar to the following snippet.

```
======================================================================
google_sql_database_instance.mysql: Still creating... [10m30s elapsed]
google_sql_database_instance.mysql: Still creating... [10m40s elapsed]
google_sql_database_instance.mysql: Still creating... [10m50s elapsed]
```

```
google_sql_database_instance.mysql: Creation complete after 10m57s
[id=book-store-db]
```

```
Apply complete! Resources: 1 added, 1 changed, 0 destroyed.
======================================================================
```

Assuming that the resources are created on the cloud, let's connect to the K8s cluster from the kubectl CLI. First, you need to have the kubeconfig file, which can be fetched from the cloud provider via various interfaces such as the CLI or UI. As you are using GCP, you fetch it via the gcloud CLI. If you use a different cloud provider, the steps differ, but they are the same once you get the kubeconfig file.

The command to generate kubeconfig in GCP via CLI is *gcloud container clusters get-credentials <K8S_CLUSTER_NAME> --region <REGION> --project <PROJECT_NAME>*

Once you get the kubeconfig file, you can create the deployment on the K8s cluster. But before proceeding to that part, let's first discuss what makes up this deployment.

- **UI**: This is the front-end part where the web-based user interface lives. It's developed in React framework, and the codebase is hosted at `https://github.com/prateek2408/BookExamples/bookStore/UI`.

- **API**: An API is a server that listens to the incoming requests and performs the desired operations required for the bookstore. The operations can be creating, listing, managing books, and so forth.

The entire application is hosted at `https://github.com/prateek2408/BookApplication`. Using the Helm chart, this application is deployed on the Kube cluster. Once the application reaches the running stage, you should see something similar to Figure 6-6.

Figure 6-6. *Sample bookstore*

The BookInfo Application

Let's look at another example and deploy a lightweight application. The motive behind deploying this application is to show how service mesh in Kubernetes can be used.

This example deploys a sample application composed of four separate microservices used to demonstrate various Istio (service mesh) features.

The application displays information about a book, similar to a single catalog entry of an online bookstore. Shown on the page is a description of the book, book details (ISBN, number of pages, and so on), and a few book reviews.

The BookInfo application is divided into four separate microservices.

- **productpage**: The product page microservice calls the details and reviews microservices to populate the page.

- **details**: This microservice contains book information.

- **reviews**: This microservice has book reviews. It also calls the ratings microservice.

- **ratings**: The ratings microservice contains book ranking information accompanying a book review.

There are three versions of the reviews microservice.

- Version v1 doesn't call the rating service.

- Version v2 calls the rating service and displays each rating as one to five black stars.

- Version v3 calls the rating service and shows each rating as one to five red stars.

The end-to-end architecture of the application is shown in Figure 6-7.

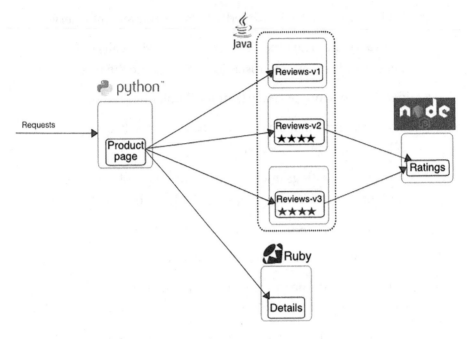

Figure 6-7. *Application overview*

This application is written in multiple languages. It's worth noting that these services have no dependencies on Istio but make an exciting service mesh example. This is because of the multitude of services, languages, and versions for the reviews service.

Setting up Istio

Follow the steps to deploy Istio on your cluster. These steps are from the official documentation of Istio at https://istio.io/latest/docs/setup/getting-started/.

Deploying the Application

To run the sample with Istio requires no changes to the application itself. Instead, you simply need to configure and run the services in an Istio-enabled environment, with Envoy sidecars injected alongside each service. The resulting deployment looks like what's shown in Figure 6-8.

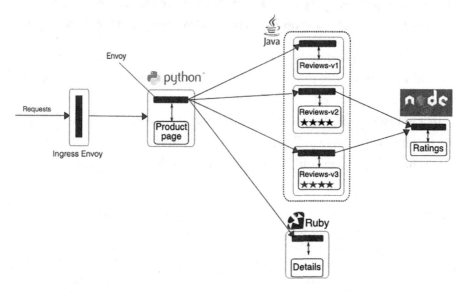

Figure 6-8. *Application traffic flow*

Sidecar Magic

All microservices are packaged with an Envoy sidecar that intercepts incoming and outgoing calls for the services, providing the hooks needed to externally control via the Istio control plane, routing, telemetry collection, and policy enforcement for the application as a whole.

Start the Application Services

If you use GKE, please ensure your cluster has at least four standard GKE nodes. If you use minikube, please ensure you have at least 4 GB RAM.

Change the directory to the root of the Istio installation.

The default Istio installation uses automatic sidecar injection. Label the namespace that hosts the application with **istio-injection=enabled**.

```
$ kubectl label namespace default istio-injection=enabled
```

Deploy your application using the kubectl command.

```
$ kubectl apply -f https://raw.githubusercontent.com/istio/
istio/release-1.13/samples/bookinfo/platform/kube/bookinfo.yaml
```

The command launches all four services shown in the BookInfo application architecture diagram. All three versions of the reviews service, v1, v2, and v3, are started.

In a realistic deployment, new microservice versions are deployed over time instead of deploying all versions simultaneously.

Confirm all services and Pods are correctly defined and running.

```
$ kubectl get services
NAME          TYPE        CLUSTER-IP    EXTERNAL-IP    PORT(S)     AGE
details       ClusterIP   10.0.0.31     <none>         9080/TCP    6m
kubernetes    ClusterIP   10.0.0.1      <none>         443/TCP     7d
productpage   ClusterIP   10.0.0.120    <none>         9080/TCP    6m
ratings       ClusterIP   10.0.0.15     <none>         9080/TCP    6m
reviews       ClusterIP   10.0.0.170    <none>         9080/TCP    6m
```

Figure 6-9.

and

```
$ kubectl get pods
NAME                             READY   STATUS    RESTARTS   AGE
details-v1-1520924117-48z17      2/2     Running   0          6m
productpage-v1-560495357-jk1lz   2/2     Running   0          6m
ratings-v1-734492171-rnr5l       2/2     Running   0          6m
reviews-v1-874083890-f0qf0       2/2     Running   0          6m
reviews-v2-1343845940-b34q5      2/2     Running   0          6m
reviews-v3-1813607990-8ch52      2/2     Running   0          6m
```

Figure 6-10.

152

To confirm that the BookInfo application is running, send a request to it by a curl command from some Pod; for example, from ratings.

```
$ kubectl exec "$(kubectl get pod -l app=ratings -o
jsonpath='{.items[0].metadata.name}')" -c ratings -- curl -sS
productpage:9080/productpage | grep -o "<title>.*</title>"
<title>Simple Bookstore App</title>
```

Apply Default Destination Rules

Destination rules in Istio help route the traffic from one microservice to another.

The following is a sample YAML that defines the destination rules for the BookInfo application.

```
apiVersion: networking.istio.io/v1alpha3
kind: DestinationRule
metadata:
  name: productpage
spec:
  host: productpage
  subsets:
  - name: v1
    labels:
      version: v1
---
apiVersion: networking.istio.io/v1alpha3
kind: DestinationRule
metadata:
  name: reviews
spec:
  host: reviews
  subsets:
```

```
  - name: v1
    labels:
      version: v1
  - name: v2
    labels:
      version: v2
  - name: v3
    labels:
      version: v3
---
apiVersion: networking.istio.io/v1alpha3
kind: DestinationRule
metadata:
  name: ratings
spec:
  host: ratings
  subsets:
  - name: v1
    labels:
      version: v1
  - name: v2
    labels:
      version: v2
---
apiVersion: networking.istio.io/v1alpha3
kind: DestinationRule
metadata:
  name: details
spec:
  host: details
  subsets:
```

```
  - name: v1
    labels:
      version: v1
  - name: v2
    labels:
      version: v2
---
```

Via the destination rules, you tell that when the traffic comes for a microservice, say ratings, then hop between multiple versions of the rating (i.e., v1, v2).

Accessing the Application

Finally, it's time to access the application via Istio Gateway. When you installed Istio, you also enabled the gateway, acting as an ingress controller. This ingress controller enables access to the bookstore.

Gateways are typically used to handle inbound traffic, but they can also manage outbound traffic. An egress gateway lets you configure a separate exit node for traffic exiting the mesh, restricting which services can access external networks or providing safe control of egress traffic to improve mesh security.

A gateway can also be used to set up an internal proxy.

Run the following commands to find out the ingress host and port.

```
export INGRESS_HOST=$(kubectl -n istio-system get service
istio-ingressgateway -o jsonpath='{.status.loadBalancer.
ingress[0].ip}')
export INGRESS_PORT=$(kubectl -n istio-system get service
istio-ingressgateway -o jsonpath='{.spec.ports[?(@.
name=="http2")].port}')
```

```
export SECURE_INGRESS_PORT=$(kubectl -n istio-system get
service istio-ingressgateway -o jsonpath='{.spec.ports[?
(@.name=="https")].port}')
export TCP_INGRESS_PORT=$(kubectl -n istio-system get service
istio-ingressgateway -o jsonpath='{.spec.ports[?
(@.name=="tcp")].port}')
```

Finally, access the application as you should see something similar to Figure 6-11.

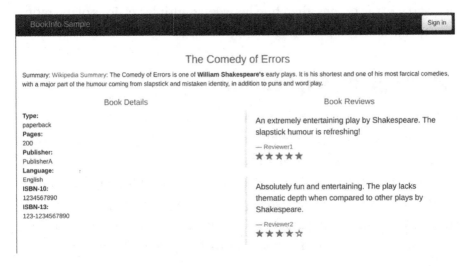

Figure 6-11. *Book information page*

Summary

All good things come to an end, and so has this book, *Kubernetes Application Developer*. I tried to cover all the details in a single place to the best of my knowledge and hope it increases your understanding. Starting from cloud computing basics to being an advanced developer in Kubernetes, you have come a long way. Cloud computing is a rapidly evolving and ever-changing domain, so the book's content might soon become outdated, but at the core, the concepts remain the same.

The book's major content is inspired by open source tooling documentation, primarily Kubernetes, Istio, Docker, and other communities. I hope you can apply the knowledge and learning imparted to you via the medium of this book. And as I stated, you are an active cloud user if you read an ebook version. :) Because this is my first book, any suggestions/feedback are greatly welcomed. I hope to write many more books related to the cloud and computing in general.

Index

© Prateek Khushalani 2022
P. Khushalani, *Kubernetes Application Developer*,
https://doi.org/10.1007/978-1-4842-8032-4

D

E

F

G

H

I

Printed in the United States
by Baker & Taylor Publisher Services